BUILDING
A CAREER

in America's
Community Colleges

Essays by Rob Jenkins

From *The Chronicle of Higher Education*

BUILDING A CAREER

in America's Community Colleges

Essays by Rob Jenkins

From *The Chronicle of Higher Education*

Community College Press®
A division of the American Association of Community Colleges
Washington, DC

The American Association of Community Colleges (AACC) is the primary advocacy organization for the nation's community colleges. The association represents more than 1,200 two-year, associate degree–granting institutions and more than 11 million students. AACC promotes community colleges through five strategic action areas: recognition and advocacy for community colleges; student access, learning, and success; community college leadership development; economic and workforce development; and global and intercultural education. Information about AACC and community colleges may be found at www.aacc.nche.edu.

The essays in this book have been adapted for republication with the permission of *The Chronicle of Higher Education.*

Designer: Brian Gallagher Design
Editor: Deanna D'Errico
Printer: Global Printing

Community College Press
American Association of Community Colleges
One Dupont Circle, NW
Suite 410
Washington, DC 20036

Printed in the United States of America.

Suggested Citation:

Jenkins, R. (2010). *Building a career in America's community colleges.* Washington, DC: Community College Press.

Library of Congress Cataloging-in-Publication Data

Jenkins, Rob (Robin David)
    Building a career in a community college: essays/by Rob Jenkins.
        p. cm.
    Includes index.
    Summary: "Collection of essays reprinted from The Chronicle of Higher Education's "Two-Year Track column." Presents sound, insider advice on building a career as a community college instructor or administrator"—Provided by publisher.
    ISBN 978-0-87117-394-2
    1. Community college teachers—Vocational guidance—United States. 2. Community college administrators—Vocational guidance—United States. I. Chronicle of higher education. II. Title.

LB1778.2.J46 2010
378.1'543023—dc22

Contents

Foreword

My job as editor of Community College Press, the publishing division of the American Association of Community Colleges (AACC), requires a lot of reading. Determining which topics are most useful to community college professionals means not only reading the proposals and manuscripts landing on my desk, but also reading widely in the field, in print and online. And, with the rapid advancement of nonprint modes of delivering content, the reading list has grown exponentially to include many electronic publications generated by and about community colleges, as well as those related to electronic publishing technology in general. So much to read, so little time: Trite but true. And I know that the same holds true for busy community college professionals.

What I've learned from all that reading, as well as from one-to-one conversations with many of our readers, is that for AACC to meet your need for more in-depth information than is available through its more frequent periodical publications (*Community College Times*, updated daily online, and *Community College Journal*, published bimonthly both in print and digitally), Community College Press needs to evolve and expand its repertoire and modes of delivery to provide you with books, monographs, and reports, print and electronic, that help you in practical and concrete ways do your jobs better. That is the new mission of Community College Press.

That brings me to the reason for publishing this book, which collects essays Rob Jenkins originally wrote for "The Two-Year Track" column in *The Chronicle of Higher Education.* Drawing on his own experience, Rob has, for many years, been dispensing much-appreciated advice from the frontline—to those considering a community college career as well as those who desire to move up the ranks.

The Press recognized the value of publishing Rob's essays for at least two reasons. One was an opportunity not to reinvent the wheel. Rob had already written useful and pertinent material—why not just be instrumental in bringing it to a wider audience? Publishing Rob's essays also presented an opportunity to enrich the community college literature through collaboration between publishers who shared an interest in advancing the community college mission: Those who learn of Rob's book from AACC will be guided to *The Chronicle*; those who learn of Rob's book from *The Chronicle* will be guided to AACC. Everybody wins.

After all, approximately 13 million students are educated in community colleges—nearly half of all U.S. undergraduates. And, as President Obama's recent White House Summit on Community Colleges underscored, community colleges play a key role in equipping the U.S. workforce with the education and training needed to support national and global economies. It is truly in the best interest of the nation to spread the word about community colleges, and I trust that this book will help.

On behalf of AACC, I wish to thank *The Chronicle of Higher Education* for unhesitatingly granting permission to share Rob's wisdom and wit with you.

Deanna D'Errico
Editor, Community College Press
American Association of Community Colleges

Preface

Late one winter afternoon in 2002, I walked into my office, tossed a stack of file folders onto my desk, plopped down in my chair, and began rubbing my temples. I had just come from a meeting of yet another faculty search committee that I was chairing, where we had culled through over 100 applications. Good grief, were they bad.

I don't mean that the candidates themselves were bad—although, admittedly, sometimes it was hard to tell. I just mean that the applications were bad. Out of all those candidates, fewer than half seemed to have any idea how to apply for any job whatsoever. One wrote his cover letter by hand on a sheet of college-ruled paper, which he then apparently tore out of his spiral notebook and stuffed into an envelope, hanging chads and all. Another included in her application materials a slim self-published volume of poetry—with a nude picture of herself on the back cover (can you say "too much information?").

Most of those who did have some idea how to apply for a job had all been groomed, apparently, to pursue endowed chairs at Harvard. Their cover letters regaled us with lengthy exegeses of their award-winning dissertations. Their CVs were full of articles "under review"—and maybe full of something else, too. Their research was all vital, seminal, and groundbreaking. Well, maybe.

You see (I wanted to tell them), we're a 2-year college. Like most 2-year colleges, we don't require our faculty members to do research or to publish. We don't even require them to have a PhD. A master's degree with 18 graduate semester hours in the teaching field will do just fine, thank you. The fact that you wrote a dissertation and have a PhD is great, but your research agenda is not what matters most to us. We're much more interested in your teaching experience. Our primary concern—what we're ultimately trying to determine—is how good a teacher you're going to be, and, not incidentally, how good a colleague.

Not only was I frustrated by the poor quality of the applications I'd just spent hours of my life poring over, but also I felt bad for those applicants. I really did want to tell them how they should go about applying for community college teaching jobs. Clearly, no one else had ever told them. I thought that perhaps, with some timely advice, I could make both their lives and mine a little better: theirs, because they might actually be able to get jobs, and mine, because I wouldn't have to look at so many awful applications year after year.

I resolved at that moment to write an essay for *The Chronicle of Higher Education* about applying for jobs at 2-year colleges, an essay like the ones I had seen on other topics in the "First Person" segment. So I looked up the editor's name and e-mail address and sent her—Denise Magner—a proposal. She responded graciously, saying she'd love to see something along those lines.

That first essay eventually morphed into three essays, which apparently were fresh enough and popular enough that I began writing for *The Chronicle* more regularly—at first, four or five times a year, then bimonthly, and finally monthly. Along the way, Denise and I created our own segment, "The Two-Year Track," where my column now runs each month.

Of course, over the years, I've broadened my horizons a bit. Writing about how to get a job at a community college is still my bread and butter, but I've also written extensively on how to prosper in that job once you've gotten it, as well as about larger issues such as tenure, diversity, and the way 2-year colleges are perceived by the public and within the profession.

The column has attracted a following over the years—as I told Denise back when we were creating "The Two-Year Track," there are a lot of community college professionals who read *The Chronicle*—and, as a result, I get a lot of e-mails from readers, most asking for job-related advice. When I discovered, a couple of years ago, that I was often referring to one or more of my columns to answer their questions, I decided it was time to pull them all together into a book. So here it is.

If you're a graduate student facing an uncertain job market, I'm hoping this book will persuade you at least to consider applying at community colleges and give you an idea how to go about it. If you've already decided that teaching at a 2-year college is the career path for you, then perhaps this book will enable you to pursue that goal more effectively. And if you're already working at a community college, I hope this book will help you to thrive and grow in that career. Whatever your situation, welcome to the 2-year track. And best wishes as you make your way along it.

Acknowledgments

First, I have to thank the two people who did the most to make this book possible: Denise Magner, my long-time editor at *The Chronicle of Higher Education*, and Deanna D'Errico at Community College Press.

Denise has done more than anyone else to help guide my writing over the past eight years, cleaning up my occasionally overwrought prose and making insightful suggestions about topics, titles, and so forth. It was Denise to whom I took my idea, about six years ago, for a special segment devoted to community college issues. She quickly saw the potential in what became known as "The Two-Year Track," which she basically created and where most of the essays in this book first appeared.

And it was Deanna who saw how all these essays fit together to make a book, and who has pushed and shepherded the manuscript through the publication process.

That said, this book would not have been possible without the unflagging support of Virginia Michelich, my friend, mentor, and—until recently—immediate supervisor. She gave me the time and the freedom to work on my *Chronicle* columns, always read them, whether she liked them or not, and never tried to tell me what I should or shouldn't write. That kind of leadership takes tremendous courage, self-confidence, and trust in others. I wish there were more administrators like her.

I'd also like to thank my good friends, colleagues, and fellow writers Jack Riggs, Marc Fitten, and Lee Jones. They always supported me in my writing, allowed me to bounce ideas off of them, often served as readers of early drafts, and more than once kept me from making a fool of myself. Thanks, too, to Debbie Riggs, who helped me prepare the final manuscript.

A special "thank you" goes to my lovely wife, Bonnie, who always shows great patience when I'm working on a column in my head (which anyone else would regard as "wool-gathering"), reads (or listens to me read) everything I ask her to, offers profound advice and criticism when I ask for it (and rarely when I don't), and laughs in all the right places. That in itself should ensure her eternal reward.

And finally, I have to thank the *Chronicle's* editor in chief, Jeff Selingo—specifically for giving me permission to use these columns in the book and more generally for recognizing the important contributions of 2-year college folks and allowing me and Denise to create special features in the magazine just for them.

Part 1

Why a Community College Career?

> I'll be the first to point out that teaching in the community college environment isn't for everyone.

TWO-YEAR COLLEGES NOT FOR YOU? THINK AGAIN

Not interested in teaching at a 2-year college? You might want to reconsider: In a typical issue of *The Chronicle of Higher Education,* more than a third of the full-time faculty positions advertised are at 2-year institutions. Even in a sluggish economy, many community colleges continue to experience record growth in enrollment, as the unemployed and underemployed seek additional training and degrees. In response to this influx of students, a surprising number of 2-year colleges are hiring new faculty members, despite drastic cuts in state budgets.

As someone who's spent a good deal of time on both sides of the hiring table— I've landed tenure-track jobs at community colleges in four state systems and served on at least a dozen search committees over the past two decades—I'll be the first to point out that teaching in the community college environment isn't for everyone. Let's face it, there are some significant drawbacks—or what many academic job-seekers might perceive as drawbacks. I'll try to outline a few of the more obvious ones here and, in the next essay, talk about why you may actually *want* to work at a community college.

The greatest downside is undoubtedly the teaching load, with its corresponding lack of time and money for research. Most 2-year colleges require a five–five load— meaning five courses each semester—and in some states it's even higher. (At several Florida colleges, for instance, the load is six courses a term.) Faculty members are also expected to serve on committees, keep regular office hours, and advise students.

None of that means you can't do research; you just have to find time, much of which will be outside the regular 40-hour-plus workweek. Nor will your scholarly efforts be entirely unappreciated. Nearly all 2-year colleges expect faculty members to engage in some sort of professional development activities, which for most means attending conferences or in-house workshops. For you, professional development could include publishing and presenting.

You should also know that money for travel is severely limited at most 2-year colleges. Some institutions support faculty travel better than others, of course, but, generally speaking you'll be lucky if you're able to attend more than one or two conferences a year, and those will probably be small local or regional gatherings. Depending on the college, you may be able to get grant money to attend one major national or international conference a year, or at least one every two or three years.

On the bright side, some faculty members find that the 2-year college environment, where there is little if any pressure to publish, affords them the opportunity to pursue research interests outside their narrow academic fields. I know of one medieval scholar, for example, who for several years has been actively presenting papers at pop-culture conferences. That sort of "branching out" might be frowned upon at a research institution, but at a community college, it's all professional development.

A second drawback, for some, may be the quality of the students. Since most 2-year colleges have open-door policies—or entrance requirements so low as to constitute de facto open-door policies—often their students aren't as well prepared for higher education as those at more selective institutions. That's not to say all community college students are underprepared. I've taught at both 4-year and 2-year colleges, and my experience has been that an average student is an average student. It's also true that a growing number of 2-year colleges have thriving honors programs, with students who would be competitive anywhere but choose to start at a community college for personal or financial reasons.

Still, the typical 2-year college does have a substantial number of weak or poorly prepared students who couldn't get into their state or regional universities. And it probably has fewer of the really top-notch students who, for some professors, make teaching worthwhile. That just comes with the territory.

OK. So maybe you can put up with the lack of research time and support, and the fact that many of your students are likely to need a great deal of extra help. But what about the pay? Again, the news here isn't exactly good—but it's not terrible, either. Two-year college faculty members tend to make substantially less over their careers than colleagues at 4-year colleges, especially those at major research universities. And you rarely find, at 2-year colleges, the kind of huge pay differentials that allow 4-year institutions to offer higher starting salaries to those in hot fields, such as science or business administration. (But that's only a drawback for people in those high-demand fields; the rest of us might see it as only fair.) On the other hand, starting salaries for community college professors are comparable to those at most 4-year colleges, especially in the humanities and social sciences—although the salary gap tends to widen over the years. And, in most state systems, professors at 2-year colleges have the same health insurance, retirement plans, and other benefits as their counterparts at 4-year campuses.

In the end, the factor that probably keeps more-qualified applicants out of the community college pool than any other is lack of prestige—whether real or perceived. Perhaps you're thinking to yourself, "I went to graduate school because I wanted to be a professor. Some of these schools don't even have academic ranks." True enough. Some 2-year colleges don't have ranks, but, to be fair, many others do.

The real question for you is, even at a 2-year college that does have ranks, are you actually going to feel like a "real" professor? Are colleagues from 4-year institutions going to take you seriously, regard you as a peer? How about your family? Your neighbors? Will they be impressed that you teach at East Podunk State Community College? The answer is, if you care that much about status, perhaps you should be looking elsewhere.

That's not to say there's no prestige at all at 2-year colleges. In many areas, these institutions are the heart and soul of the community, the local center for the arts and sciences and anything else smacking of sophistication. College faculty members, by extension, are often regarded as the most knowledgeable people around in their respective fields. They can also become well respected within the 2-year-college community, a vast network of institutions and scholars with its own set of journals, professional conferences, and other events.

The bottom line, though, is that a teaching career at a 2-year college is primarily about just that—teaching. Not prestige. Not grant acquisition. Not scholarship. Just teaching. And that's not a drawback. It's the best thing about the job.

The original essay was published October 21, 2003, in *The Chronicle of Higher Education*.

Teaching at a 2-year college actually has a lot of
advantages over teaching at a 4-year institution.

NOT A BAD GIG

Teaching at a 2-year college actually has a lot of advantages over teaching at a 4-year institution—and certainly over being unemployed. In my first essay about teaching careers at community colleges, I focused mostly on the bad news: heavy teaching loads, little time for research, underprepared students, lower salaries, lack of prestige. If my frankness made some think twice about applying for openings at 2-year colleges, well, good. I've sat across the table from too many candidates who had no idea what a community college was all about, and who probably wouldn't have been there if they had.

But bad news, of course, is hardly the whole story. First and foremost among the advantages is job security. I know you can have job security at a 4-year institution, too—provided you get tenure, which can be more or less difficult depending on the institution. It's also true that not all 2-year colleges offer tenure, or, as some call it, a "continuing contract."

But most community colleges do offer some version of tenure—and it's often relatively easy to get. Unlike their counterparts at 4-year institutions, who may be required to publish numerous articles and perhaps even a book to be considered for tenure, community college faculty members have no such mandate. The truth is, at most 2-year colleges, you don't have to publish anything to get tenure. You will probably be expected to participate in some sort of professional development, but that could mean something as simple as attending technology-training sessions on the campus and going to the occasional academic conference. While those are useful and worthwhile activities, they're clearly not as demanding as writing a book.

More importantly, you will certainly have to show evidence of good teaching and also, in most cases, of service to the institution, because those are the primary activities of community college faculty members. But if you're able to do that—if you can document that you've consistently been a good teacher, that you've served on committees and performed other important functions for the college, and that you've undergone at least some professional development—you can probably get tenure at most 2-year colleges in 3 to 5 years—7 at the outside.

Another potential advantage of the "teaching track" is that you don't have to have a terminal degree. Read the ads for faculty positions at community colleges, and you'll see that nearly all list the same minimum requirements: master's degree with 18 graduate semester hours in your particular field. Don't assume that the term "minimum requirement" implies that those with a master's degree don't stand a chance. Two-year colleges actually hire lots of people with "just a master's"—two thirds or more of the faculty at many 2-year institutions hold only a master's. True, some of those faculty members are A.B.D. [all but dissertation], and many others have hours beyond the master's. Quite a few go on to earn additional graduate hours—in many cases, at the college's expense—and some even complete their terminal degrees. But they were hired with "just a master's."

Does that mean PhDs need not apply? Certainly not. In fact, in recent years, the trend at community colleges has been to hire more PhDs, partly because the market is glutted with them and partly, perhaps, because word has gotten out that a community college can be a pretty nice place to work. My college, this past year, hired 16 new tenure-track faculty members, 6 of whom hold terminal degrees. Ten years ago, only two or three of the new hires would have had them.

That said, I don't believe that a terminal degree will necessarily give you an advantage in applying or interviewing. The faculty search committees I've served on—at least a dozen in the past decade—were looking for the best teachers we could find. Sometimes they were people with PhDs, sometimes not. Our hiring committees tend to be "degree blind," especially in the final stages of the search process.

Another advantage has to do with quality-of-life issues. In addition to less stress, since faculty members probably won't perish if they don't publish, community college teaching offers other lifestyle benefits, some quite tangible. It's true that, on average, faculty salaries at 2-year colleges tend to be lower than those at 4-year institutions—in some cases, much lower. On the other hand, 2-year colleges are often located in areas where the cost of living is significantly lower than the national (or at least the state) average. Many community college professors are able to live quite comfortably, despite the lower salaries. In addition, most state systems offer excellent insurance coverage, including health, dental, vision, and life, along with a generous retirement plan. Many also allow faculty members to take graduate courses within the state system at no cost, and some even provide tuition benefits for their spouses and children.

Prestige? That—what there is of it—is part of the package, too. Over the years, I've known many colleagues who were highly regarded in their local communities as experts. A friend of mine, a history professor, published a popular history of the area where he lives. A political science professor I know is frequently quoted in the local news media. Others sponsor book clubs, give lectures to community art and literary groups, or write columns for the newspaper.

Ultimately, though, the best thing about teaching at a 2-year school is just that: teaching. That's our primary mission, and we know it. We embrace it. Our students know it, too, and they expect us to be good at it. By and large, we are very good at it—especially given the fact that so many of our students are less than ready for college when they arrive. If there's anything more rewarding in this profession than introducing a bright yet poorly prepared (and perhaps unmotivated) student to the joy of learning, perhaps for the first time, I haven't encountered it. All teachers get to experience that occasionally. Community college teachers do it every day.

So, yes, my colleagues at 4-year institutions are publishing a lot more than I am. Some of them are even becoming famous, or at least well known in their fields. Their paychecks certainly have bigger numbers before the decimal point. But I seriously doubt that their careers—or their lives, for that matter—are any more fulfilling than mine.

The original essay was published November 10, 2003, in *The Chronicle of Higher Education*.

So just who are community college students, anyway?
I decided to play amateur sociologist and explore that question
by touring the parking lot at my large suburban 2-year campus.
The results, at first, were a bit surprising.

KNOW THY STUDENTS

"Know thyself," Socrates famously advised, while Sun Tzu counseled prospective warriors, "Know thine enemy." To those legendary admonitions, I would add this one, aimed at anyone beginning or considering a career in 2-year college teaching: "Know thy students."

So just who are community college students, anyway? I decided to play amateur sociologist and explore that question by touring the parking lot at my large suburban 2-year campus. The results, at first, were a bit surprising.

From the automobile sample I examined—in which, by the way, 10-year-old Hondas and Toyotas were disproportionately represented—I determined that our students tend to come from the lower half of the economic spectrum, that they lean to the left politically (judging by the bumper stickers), and that many of them are struggling to raise young families (car seats were visible in approximately a third of the vehicles). Then I realized I was in the faculty parking lot.

The student lot, however, was even more eye-opening: everything from Lexus SUVs to rusted and sagging sedans of indeterminate age and origin, from pick-up trucks to hybrids. Bumper stickers ranged from "Choose Life" to "War Is Not the Answer." (Not that those are necessarily mutually exclusive sentiments.) And yes, a goodly number of car seats were in evidence.

All of which told me exactly what I already knew: Two-year college students are such a marvelously diverse group, they can hardly be called a "group" at all. Demographers may tell us that the typical community college student is a 27-year-old woman with 2.5 kids, but beyond that rather meaningless statistical analysis, there really is no "typical" community college student. That's because 2-year colleges are the most egalitarian of postsecondary institutions. Almost anybody can attend a community college, and almost anybody does.

Still, there is much that 2-year-college instructors and aspiring instructors can learn about the people who will inhabit their classrooms—some of it expected, some not. In fact, the truth about community college students often flies in the face of long-established stereotypes. For example, it's an article of faith in certain academic circles that students who gravitate toward 2-year colleges couldn't hack it at a "real college." Like most misconceptions, that belief is based on an element of truth. It's certainly true that our students, on average, have lower SAT and ACT scores than their counterparts at 4-year institutions. The fact that so many 2-year colleges have "open door" policies—meaning that they admit anyone with a high school diploma or GED—virtually guarantees that disparity.

Another predictable result of open-door policies is that many new students at community colleges are not prepared for college-level work. In fact, at a typical 2-year college, 30% to 40% of first-year students enroll in precollegiate courses (also known as remedial or developmental courses), based on standardized placement test scores. None of that should be terribly surprising, given that the mission of the community college is basically to provide access to higher education for those who might not otherwise have it. If you teach at a community college, you can reasonably expect to have students in your classes who struggle to read, write, and compute at a college level. And if your discipline is English or math, you may even be called upon to teach developmental courses. (And maybe you'll discover that you enjoy it, although that's a topic for another essay.)

But what I've found surprising, during my 18-year teaching career in the community college arena, is not how many of my students aren't well prepared for college, but how many of them are. One of the best-kept secrets in higher education today is the proliferation of honors programs at 2-year colleges. Those programs are designed to accommodate students whose SAT scores would allow them to get into "prestigious" colleges, but who find themselves at a community college for any number of personal reasons. Classes in those honors programs tend to be smaller, the curriculum more in-depth, and the instruction more focused on class discussion and collaboration than most courses. The purpose isn't so much to "improve" the student body by attracting "better" students—community colleges don't tend to think that way—but rather to better serve *all* students: the academically gifted as well as the underprepared. (It's worth noting that few if any 2-year colleges offer enough honors courses to satisfy all of a student's core requirements, meaning that such students take many of their classes with the general student population. In other words, they will be sitting in your classroom, right alongside students fresh from remediation. Therein lies the challenge of community college teaching.)

In addition to students who place into developmental and honors programs, community colleges have plenty of just plain ordinary students—those who might not have been able to get into the state's flagship university but who certainly would have been admitted to a small regional college. For many of those students, the local community college is an attractive alternative, because of its low cost, proximity to home, or popular programs. Tuition is often two thirds or even half what students would pay at a 4-year college. And they can usually cut expenses even further by living at home. Because most 2-year colleges are part of state systems that allow easy transfer of credits among institutions, students can stay close to home for an extra year or two, take the core courses they need while they figure out what they want to study, then transfer to a 4-year institution when they're ready.

That is, *if* they transfer. A large number of students on a typical community college campus have no intention of transferring to a 4-year campus. They are attending a community college for one of its popular 2-year degree programs, such as nursing or information technology. Here again, the notion that those students must not be as intellectually gifted as their transfer-oriented peers is simply, in most cases, mistaken. Nursing students, in particular, tend to be among the most intelligent and driven students on the campus, because nursing programs at most 2-year colleges are highly selective.

Another misconception about community college students is that they're primarily "returning" students—i.e., older. While it's certainly true that the average age at a typical 2-year college is significantly higher than at most 4-year institutions—around 28 at my institution, for instance—we also serve our fair share of "traditional age" students, meaning 18- and 19-year-olds.

The truth is, students of traditional college age make up a large and growing segment of the 2-year student population. As Clifford Adelman recently discovered in his landmark study *Moving Into Town—and Moving On: The Community College in the Lives of Traditional Age Students,* 42% of community college students are now under the age of 22—an increase of 10 percentage points in the last decade. That statistic doesn't mean your students will be any better or any worse, just that they might be a little different from what you've been led to expect.

And that's my point. Community college students are young and old, male and female, rich and poor, Black and White (and Asian and Hispanic and Native American). They're gifted and needy, Republican and Democrat, urban and rural.

Perhaps as a graduate student you envisioned yourself imparting knowledge to the best and brightest at one of the nation's elite institutions. Now you're teaching at a community college, or contemplating doing so. Some might see that as "settling," but you don't have to look at it that way. You can still impart knowledge to the best and brightest—along with the disadvantaged, the statistically average, and the woefully underprepared.

Even better, as you immerse yourself in the richness and diversity that characterize the community college classroom, you will discover that your students also impart knowledge to you: knowledge about a wide range of economic situations, family circumstances, and cultural backgrounds. And along the way, you may even learn something important about yourself: that you enjoy being here, in this job, with these students. Socrates would be proud.

References

Adelman, C. (2005, February). *Moving into town—and moving on: The community college in the lives of traditional age students.* Washington, DC: U.S. Department of Education.

The original essay was published September 27, 2005, in *The Chronicle of Higher Education.*

The truth is, the typical community college campus these days looks, demographically, a lot like the typical 4-year campus.

ZEN AND THE ART OF COMMUNITY COLLEGE BASHING

Personally, I wasn't as offended as some of my colleagues by Peter Onear's essay, "An Enlightening Trip to the Countryside," in which he described in smug terms his visit to a suburban community college not far from his own urban 4-year campus. Like so many who have spent their careers in the academic backwater of Community Collegeville, I live for the occasional pat on the head. If I'm ever fortunate enough to meet Mr. "Onear," I plan on asking for his autograph, and maybe a bedtime story.

Sarcasm aside, I do recognize that Onear, a government-relations officer at a large university, probably meant well. No doubt, from his admittedly comfortable perch atop the academic food chain, he felt he was being complimentary, even magnanimous, when he alluded to the "attractive campus" of the 2-year college he visited, and insisted that those of us who toil in such places are "doing God's work."

Unfortunately, Onear's condescending tone and constant reliance on stereotypes lead me to conclude that his trip wasn't nearly enlightening enough. Or at least it wasn't for him. For those of us actually engaged in "God's work," his column ought to be very enlightening indeed, as it reminds us we still have much to do in fighting false perceptions about community colleges.

Where to begin cataloging Onear's ill-informed statements, biased assumptions, and patronizing prattle? Let's start with the obvious: One need not be a social scientist to realize his conclusions are fundamentally flawed, based as they are on a sample of one. Because Onear never mentions any other such road trips—indeed, he sounds for much of the essay as if he's never seen a 2-year campus before— his perceptions of community colleges in general appear to arise from a single encounter.

For example, he tells us after touring the institution in question that "community college campuses aren't happy-go-lucky places," and declares that there's a "certain grimness" about them. Grimness? Really? What exactly does he mean by that? That students aren't throwing Frisbees on the lawn between classes? That they're not whooping it up on fraternity row after an all-night kegger? That they're not tearing down the goal posts when the football team wins a big game?

Speaking as someone who has worked at five 2-year colleges and visited dozens more, I can honestly say that the word "grim" has never entered my mind in connection with any of them. It may be true, as Onear says, that "students at 2-year colleges are serious and purposeful"—although not all of them, and not all of the time—but it's certainly not true that, in general, they "have neither the time nor desire to hang out at the student union." In my 21 years of teaching at 2-year colleges, I've seen lots of my students "hanging out" in the student center, not to mention throwing Frisbees on the lawn. I might even characterize a few of them as borderline happy-go-lucky.

Onear's observations regarding relative institutional size are also rather misleading. By describing his visit to one institution with "about 5000 full- and part-time students," he might leave some readers with the impression that all community colleges tend to operate on a smaller scale than universities. He notes that "it's easier for an institution to handle 5,000 students than 25,000 . . . [and] to work with a few dozen faculty members than a few hundred." While there are certainly many 2-year colleges with 5,000 or fewer students (just as there are many 4-year institutions in that range), some are actually a bit larger than his own cherished university.

In fact, according to the 2008 *Digest of Education Statistics* (Snyder, Dillow, & Hoffman, 2009, Table 236), of the 120 largest degree-granting institutions in the country, 23 are 2-year colleges. Miami Dade College is the third-largest institution of any type, with more than 51,000 students. The Houston Community College system serves nearly 43,000. Nine others have 30,000 or more. And I'm guessing each of them employs more than a few dozen faculty members. [Note: Statistics are updated since original publication of essay.]

Onear's most startling assertion, by far, is "that most students at community colleges are enrolled there only because (1) their parents and/or spouses are insisting on it; (2) they are unemployed or minimally employed and desperately need some education; or (3) their bosses are making them take classes to stay employed." In other words, no one in his or her right mind would attend a community college unless he or she positively had to.

Wow. If that were even close to being true, 2-year colleges would indeed be pretty grim places. Fortunately, it's not, and they're not. The truth is, the typical community college campus these days looks, demographically, a lot like the typical 4-year campus. Certainly, we serve a fair number of disadvantaged students who don't have much money, along with many students who are academically underprepared, and a healthy dose of adult students returning to school. We do so proudly. (It is God's work, after all.)

However, according to statistics compiled by the American Association of Community Colleges (AACC; 2010a, 2010b), the average age of 2-year students has been trending sharply downward in recent years, meaning that we are now enrolling many of the students who used to end up at midsize state universities—or even, in some cases, the big research institutions. That's partly because of money, as Onear suggests. But really it's more about value, which is to say the intersection between cost and quality. What people like Onear fail to recognize is that, these days, lots of students go to community colleges because they've figured out they can get a high-quality education there—in smaller classes, taught by actual professors instead of graduate students—for a fraction of the cost. They've also learned that they can transfer to 4-year institutions, if that's what they want to do, and be very competitive.

In other words, community colleges are no longer just for students who can't go anywhere else, if indeed we ever were. We've become a major portal for all kinds of students to enter higher education. And all kinds of students are doing so in record numbers: Nearly half of all U.S. undergraduates attend 2-year colleges, according to AACC (2010a). That, of course, is a message we have been trying to convey for years, and one that finally appears (from my vantage point, at least) to be taking hold. But you would never know that from reading Onear, who seems content with recycling the tired stereotypes of decades past. I understand that in doing so he doesn't intend to demean community colleges, or those who attend them, or those who work there, but—well, you know what they say about good intentions. Try not to hold it against him, though. Instead, just think of him as unenlightened.

References

American Association of Community Colleges. (2010a). *Fast facts.* Available from http://www.aacc.nche.edu/aboutcc/pages/fastfacts.aspx

American Association of Community Colleges. (2010b). *Students at community colleges.* Available from http://www.aacc.nche.edu/aboutcc/trends/pages/studentsat-communitycolleges.aspx

Onear, P. (2008, March 6). An enlightening trip to the countryside. *The Chronicle* of *Higher Education.* Available from http://www.chroniclecareers.com/article/an-enlightening-trip-to-the/45723/

Snyder, T. D., Dillow, S. A., & Hoffman, C. M. (2009, March). *Digest of education statistics: 2008* (NCES 2009-020). Washington, DC: U.S. Department of Education, National Center for Education Statistics.

The original essay was published April 9, 2008, in *The Chronicle of Higher Education.*

> By changing our own attitudes and behaviors, administrators and faculty members can begin to alter the perception that 2-year colleges are less rigorous and intellectually stimulating than 4-year institutions.

NO MORE 13TH GRADE

"Paddy High." That's what students called the college behind our backs. As a new faculty member at Alabama Southern Community College in the mid-1990s, I wondered about that strange epithet. Then a veteran colleague clued me in: After the campus was founded as Patrick Henry State Junior College, in 1965, local wags lost no time dubbing it Patrick Henry High School, or Paddy High for short—a commentary on the fledgling institution's perceived lack of status. Thirty years and a name change later, the label still stuck—along with the community's misconceptions about 2-year colleges.

The reality, of course, is quite different. Alabama Southern was recognized by the Ford Foundation in 1994 as one of the nation's most innovative community colleges. In 2005 it won a National Bellwether Award for Instructional Excellence. Other 2-year colleges where I've worked, including my current institution, have earned similar accolades. Yet I've heard students disparage them all, referring dismissively to their first-year experience as "13th grade": a bit more demanding than high school, perhaps, but nothing like a "real" university. Or so they imagine, most of them having never set foot on a university campus except maybe to attend athletics events.

Since those of us who work at 2-year colleges know better, we tend to bristle at such ignorant and callous remarks. Yet we may be the very people whose actions and attitudes unwittingly reinforce the negative stereotypes. That's been my observation as I've visited various 2-year colleges and corresponded with colleagues across the country. One thing is certain: If the public perceptions of community colleges as mere extensions of high school are ever going to change, the responsibility for bringing about that change rests squarely on our shoulders.

Let's start with administrators (since I've been one, in some form or another, for the past 15 years). If some community colleges seem to be little more than glorified high schools, perhaps that's because administrators tend to think of them that way. They have what I refer to as a "high school mentality." To understand that mentality, and the problems it poses for a college, consider the main difference between high school and college from a faculty point of view—namely, the degree of autonomy.

Typically high school teachers are bound by a rigid schedule and a strictly mandated workweek. They must arrive by a certain time each morning and stay until a certain time each afternoon. In between they're required to be at their various "work-stations"—classroom, cafeteria, bus line—for specified periods. Only teachers who conform to those expectations are "doing their jobs." Others risk disciplinary action.

College professors, on the other hand, often gravitate toward postsecondary teaching precisely because we seek to avoid that kind of stifling work environment. We prefer to arrange our schedules around our personal and professional needs. We want to teach classes, keep office hours, attend committee meetings, and then leave when we're done—usually so we can go home and grade papers or work on other projects—rather than stick around until 5 p.m. to satisfy some administrator's notion of a standard workweek.

At many community colleges, however, the 40-hour week, meaning 40 hours on the campus, is the administration's main tool for gauging faculty productivity. Those administrators apparently don't take into account that many faculty members at 2-year colleges actually work 50 or 60 hours a week. Nor do those administrators seem to care that, in many cases, we can get more work done at home than in the office. In their minds, if faculty members aren't standing in front of classrooms or sitting in their offices, they're not working. That's the high school mentality at its worst.

Another area in which high school teachers have little or no autonomy is in choosing textbooks and making other decisions about the curriculum. Usually curriculum at the secondary-school level is developed by systemwide "curriculum specialists," with books chosen by administrators or, at best, by large committees. Individual faculty members have little or no input, and the concept of academic freedom does not apply.

For college professors, though, teaching is all about academic freedom. We prefer broad course outlines, which leave a great deal of latitude for each instructor to decide how to approach topics in class. And we like to choose our own textbooks or, if textbook selection is a departmental decision, we at least expect to have a say in which books are used.

Unfortunately, at many community colleges, the trend among administrators is toward standardizing the curriculum to "ensure quality"—even though taking those decisions out of the hands of faculty members probably accomplishes exactly the opposite. Some administrators also mandate textbook choices to accommodate students (they say) and, increasingly, to accommodate booksellers (something they don't say).

The problem is that when administrators treat professors like high school teachers—checking up on us during the "work day," insisting that we adhere to antiquated schedules, usurping our authority over the curriculum—those not-so-subtle signs are not lost on students. It's no wonder they think they're still in high school. Conversely, when administrators acknowledge community college faculty members as professionals, that has a trickle-down effect on students. Eventually, as the attitude of the institution toward its faculty members becomes apparent, students come to view their professors—and by extension the college—with more respect.

But let's not place all of the blame on administrators. Sometimes it's faculty members who behave as if we work at a high school. And again it's no wonder students don't regard us as real professors when, all too often, we fail to live up to the title. Consider professional development. How many faculty members reading this column—and exclaiming "Right on, brother" every time I criticize administrators—have engaged in any serious professional development activities in the past year? How many have done more than just attend a conference or two? How many have presented a paper, written a journal article, reviewed a book? More to the point, how many of you have taken serious inventory of your own teaching, perhaps exploring new technologies and methodologies to improve your performance in the classroom? How many of you regularly peruse the journals in your field, keeping up not only with developments in the discipline but also with new ideas about pedagogy?

As a group, community college professors don't always approach such activities with enthusiasm. We're busy. We teach five or six classes a semester. We have loads of papers to grade, meetings to attend, committees to chair. And so we let the extras slide. Yet those so-called extras form the very definition of the word *professor*. Sure, faculty members at community colleges teach a lot—we work at teaching institutions, after all. But a professor is more than just a teacher. A professor is a lifelong student, not only of his or her field but also of teaching itself. A professor is a writer, a researcher, and a scholar—even if only in a small way.

In truth, faculty members at 2-year colleges who merely put in their time before going home at 5 p.m. (OK, 4 p.m.) *are* little different from high school teachers. They're not behaving like professors, so why should students regard them as such? On the other hand, faculty members who are visibly engaged with their subject matter are more likely to gain the respect of their students. So are those who take time to learn the newest classroom technology and stay abreast of the latest pedagogical developments, identifying what works best for them and adapting it to their teaching. That's what students expect when they come to college, and what they have a right to expect: not 9-to-5ers, but true professors, living the life of the mind, even if much of their time is spent on mundane tasks.

By changing our own attitudes and behaviors, administrators and faculty members can begin to alter the perception that 2-year colleges are less rigorous and intellectually stimulating than 4-year institutions. We can help students appreciate more fully the value of a community college education, whether they plan to enter the work force or transfer. Most important, we can develop a sense of pride in ourselves and our institutions that will carry over to the communities we serve. Because the fact is, we're not the 13th grade. Community colleges open the doors of higher education to students for whom those doors would otherwise be closed. And that's something no high school, and very few universities, can say.

The original essay was published December 16, 2008, in *The Chronicle of Higher Education.*

Having a doctorate doesn't automatically make someone a better teacher of freshmen and sophomores, and to suggest otherwise is absurd.

CALL ME RUBE

Please, don't call me "doctor." I don't have a PhD, an EdD, an MD, a PsyD, a JD, a HumD, a DD, or, to my knowledge, ADD. There. Let that serve as a blanket correction to all who have addressed me over the years as "Dr. Jenkins," no doubt because of the various teaching and administrative positions I've held.

Some, like students, either don't realize that I'm "just" an MA or else don't understand the difference. Others—mostly job applicants—operate under the very reasonable assumption that someone who doesn't hold a doctorate probably won't take offense at being addressed as "doctor," while someone who does probably will be offended if the title is omitted. (I've always operated under that assumption myself, having generally found it to be true.)

Of course, I correct people on the spot when I can do so without causing them embarrassment or derailing the conversation. Otherwise, I look for an opportunity to clarify my status at some later point in our relationship. And I always try to make it clear to my students, at the beginning of each term, that it's "Mr. Jenkins" or "Professor Jenkins." Or, if they prefer, they can simply call me "Master."

What I am about to say here is not intended as an antidoctorate screed. Hey, some of my best friends are PhDs. More important, I spent enough time in a PhD program to know that completing a doctorate of any type is a monumental achievement, and I have great respect for those who've done it. I just don't feel inferior to them, either intellectually, professionally, or socially—any more than I feel inferior to my good friend who happens to be an OB/GYN and makes three times as much money as I do. He decided what he wanted to do in life and then obtained the education he needed to achieve that goal. I did the same thing.

That's why I'm troubled by what I see as a growing infatuation, among community colleges, with the PhD—sometimes to the exclusion of highly qualified candidates with an MA, who might be better teachers. A handful of 2-year colleges around the country are actually insisting on the terminal degree, while many others are actively working to increase the percentage of their faculty members who have doctorates. No doubt the trend is fueled, in part, by the recent influx of PhDs into a very tight job market. There are simply more candidates with doctorates out there, and more of them seem willing to consider teaching at a community college. By and large, that's probably a good thing.

The problem lies with the colleges themselves. Why is it that they want to hire more PhDs, after all? To raise their prestige in the community or impress sister institutions? To brag about their numbers in their annual reports? Or do they genuinely believe that having a PhD makes someone a better teacher? Obviously, some people feel that way. A recent poster on one of *The Chronicle's* blogs had this to say: "College was supposed to be 'higher' education because the instruction came from the producers of knowledge and not just some rube with a master's degree." Sounds to me like somebody has a bit of a God complex.

That aside, the assertion that someone with "just a master's" isn't qualified to teach introductory college courses deserves a rebuttal. Let's start by acknowledging that, in the traditional hierarchy of graduate education, a master's is the teaching degree. (The word *master* even comes from the Latin word *magister,* which means *teacher.*) Recipients of the degree have mastered their content areas and are therefore, by definition, competent to teach in those areas. The doctorate, by comparison, is a research degree. Of course, most people who hold doctorates also have master's degrees (or the equivalent), so they're clearly qualified to teach as well as to conduct research. But the doctorate itself doesn't make them any more qualified to do the former, at least in lower-division courses.

In other words, having a doctorate doesn't automatically make someone a better teacher of freshmen and sophomores, and to suggest otherwise is absurd. If you're a research chemist, you might well be a "producer of knowledge" in the sense that you're constantly discovering new things about the narrow area of chemistry you're studying. But that knowledge probably has little or no relation to your first-and second-year chemistry courses. That is, if you even teach entry-level courses. Because, let's be honest, many researchers don't. At the vast majority of Research I institutions, the teaching of introductory classes is the sole province of the graduate students, who are, well, rubes with master's degrees, I guess.

But I digress. The question was whether someone needs a PhD to teach at a community college, and to that I answer: no, of course not. Two-year colleges are almost exclusively teaching institutions, and for faculty members at a teaching institution, a teaching degree should be quite enough. In fact, most of the MAs I've worked with obtained that degree specifically because that's what they wanted to do: teach.

Consider my case. I went to graduate school intending to earn a PhD and become a literary theorist. Along the way, I figured out that what I really wanted to do was teach composition. After completing my MA, and the course work for the PhD, I decided I had all the formal education I needed and went out and got a job. Twenty-three years later, I have absolutely no regrets.

Would finishing my doctorate all those years ago have made me a better teacher today? I honestly don't see how. A slightly better-paid teacher, perhaps, but not more competent. The best training I've received has been in the classroom. The 20 or 30 courses I taught during the time it would have taken me to write a dissertation were far more valuable to me professionally than an obscure monograph collecting dust in a library.

I'm not saying that having a doctorate makes someone a worse teacher. Clearly, there are good and bad teachers on both sides of the PhD line. My experience interviewing and supervising PhDs over the years suggests that, on average, they're more interested in research than in teaching—which is probably why they pursued a PhD to begin with—but of course, that's a pretty broad generalization. Most of the great teachers who inspired me when I was an undergraduate and a graduate student held doctorates, and since then, I've worked beside many PhDs cut from the same cloth. The problem arises when administrators and hiring committees at 2-year colleges assume that job candidates with PhDs are more qualified for a faculty position just because they have doctorates. That's rarely the case, and such assumptions can cause us to overlook some truly outstanding, committed teachers who have "just a master's."

Readers often ask me if they need to finish a doctorate in order to teach at a community college. I tell them, "If you have a burning desire to get a doctorate, or will feel incomplete without one, then get one. If you want to go into upper administration or teach at a 4-year college one day, then get one. But if what you really want to do is teach at a community college, the master's is all you need." I believe that's sound advice, and I would hope that most of my colleagues—especially those who serve on search committees—would agree. After all, you know what they say: The more rubes, the merrier.

The original essay was published May 6, 2009, in *The Chronicle of Higher Education.*

> I get to do what I love every day: interact with students, teach writing, and engage in stimulating conversations with my colleagues. Those are the things I envisioned myself doing when I set out to become a college professor nearly 30 years ago.

THE DISCOUNT PROFESSORSHIP

Ever since I saw Jimmy Stewart in *The Rare Breed* as a kid, I've always wanted to be described in those same words. Now, if Melanie Benson is right about the current state of the professoriate, I may have finally achieved my goal: I'm a midcareer associate professor who makes a decent living, owns a home, and has never had any student-loan debt. Benson, an assistant professor of Native American studies at Dartmouth College, published an essay in *The Chronicle of Higher Education* ("At What Cost?") lamenting the fact that her professional accomplishments have not led to commensurate financial success. Even with an Ivy League salary, she finds the cost of living in her part of the country oppressive. She doesn't think she'll ever be able to afford a home. The monthly payments on the debt she accumulated as a student are bleeding her dry.

I sympathize with Benson, partly because she reminds me of friends of mine who borrowed heavily to finance careers in fields that are not particularly high-paying. But I'd like to point out—and I don't mean this unkindly—that her predicament is largely of her own creation, the result of choices she made. I'm not saying they were bad choices or that she was wrong to make them. That's not for me to judge. I'm just stating the obvious: They were choices, and she made them. And choices have consequences, both positive and negative. On the plus side, Benson has an enviable position at one of the world's great colleges, a result of having attended all the right institutions and done extraordinarily well. On the down side, the cost of all that prestige has been a crippling student-loan debt that will likely weigh on her for years.

To those who read Benson's essay and wondered if a career in academe was really worth the cost, I would suggest that there is another way to go about it. I'm not saying it's a better way, just different. And I can vouch for it because it's the route to the professoriate that I took.

I began my career on a partial academic and athletic scholarship—"partial" meaning that it covered less than half of my expenses—at a small but prestigious liberal arts college. My parents couldn't really afford to help me out much, but that first year I was able to make up the difference with some cash I had saved. It seemed like a great situation: I was at a good college, receiving a "quality education," playing a sport I loved.

During my second semester, though, reality began to intrude on my idyllic fantasy. After a season of competing against college-level athletes, I realized I didn't have much future in that arena (pardon the bad pun). It also became clear that, in order to return for the next three or four years, I was going to have to borrow money. A lot of money. It didn't seem worth it.

So I transferred to a nearby midsize state university, where I could afford the tuition and living expenses through a combination of financial aid and part-time jobs. Neither the institution nor the English department at the university was highly regarded (the campus itself was actually a notorious "party school"), but I studied hard, got to know my professors, and learned everything I could from them. When it came time to apply for graduate school, I had high grades, solid GRE scores, and stellar recommendations.

On the advice of my major adviser, I applied to five graduate programs: three top-tier programs and two fallback ones. I was accepted at all five. But none of the top-tier departments offered me any financial assistance, while both of the fallback ones did. Clearly, I had another decision to make.

I say that now but, looking back, I don't think I ever seriously considered borrowing tens of thousands of dollars to get a graduate degree in English, even from a top-tier university. It just didn't seem to make much sense. If I'd been going to law school (which I briefly considered), I might have done that. At least as a lawyer, I could reasonably expect to make enough money to pay off those loans without having to live on oatmeal and ramen noodles. But as an English teacher? No way. I would barely be able to afford a used copy of *101 Things to Do with Ramen Noodles*. So off I went to Fallback U. It awarded me a fellowship and, later, a graduate assistantship that paid all my tuition and provided a small stipend to boot.

Once there, I learned a couple of interesting things. One was that my undergraduate "party school" had actually prepared me pretty well for graduate study. I was at least as well prepared as any of my classmates, including a few who came from top-tier undergraduate institutions. I also learned that Fallback U. had a pretty good graduate program in its own right. I enjoyed the professors, the environment, and my fellow students. Best of all, although I was certainly poor at that time, I wasn't overly burdened by debt. I had made the right choice.

As my studies continued, however, another choice began to loom. I was close to finishing the PhD course work when my wife and I discovered she was pregnant. I could stay in school another three or four years, finish the PhD, and borrow money to live on, or I could get a job. I elected to get a job.

Of course the only teaching job I could get in my field without a PhD wasn't exactly at Dartmouth. It was at a community college. And even back then, in the mid-1980s, I was fortunate to get it. (I was also offered a job writing reports for a government agency that actually paid better than the teaching gig. I passed.)

That was 23 years ago. As I look back, I can honestly find little to regret, even though my choices, like Benson's, have led to some negative consequences—or at least to what some people might regard as negative. For one thing, I've been "stuck" in community colleges my entire career. That has meant heavy teaching loads, comparatively low pay (compared to Dartmouth, at least), and virtually no professional prestige within the higher education community. In fact, I bet some of you reading this are saying to yourselves, "Well, he's not a *real* professor." That's why many academics would rather sell their souls than teach at a community college, and quite a few probably have.

My decision to leave graduate school without finishing the PhD isn't something I would necessarily recommend to anyone else—although, as I've written before, if what you want to do is teach at a community college, you don't really need a doctorate. Still, I've been limited somewhat by that decision, in that I'll probably never be able to hold a permanent high-level administrative post (even though I served as interim academic dean for a year) or teach at a 4-year college. Fortunately, I don't really care to do either of those things.

Also on the bright side is the fact that I get to do what I love every day: interact with students, teach writing, and engage in stimulating conversations with my colleagues. Those are the things I envisioned myself doing when I set out to become a college professor nearly 30 years ago. Moreover, my job offers great benefits and a decent salary that, if not up to Ivy League standards, at least allows me to own a nice home in a pleasant suburb with good schools, parks, and libraries—a circumstance that is also due, in large part, to the region of the country where I've chosen to live (hint: not the Northeast or the West Coast).

So there is a less-expensive path to the professoriate, yet, given the state of the job market in the humanities, I wouldn't encourage students to follow even the cheaper route at this time. The reality is that many of you reading this are unable to find any kind of full-time teaching job in academe. Others, just as capable and at least as well educated as I, teach part time at two or three different campuses, trying to cobble together a meager living. Believe me, I know how blessed I am. I have a son in college now, and I advised him not to pursue a faculty career in higher education, despite the satisfaction that it has brought me.

But if you know those truths and you still want to pursue a faculty career in academe, all I'm saying is, you don't have to mortgage your future to do so. You can if you want, and it may work out for you, as it has (to some extent) for Melanie Benson. But if the cost of a professorship seems too high, just remember: You can probably get it at a discount.

References

Benson, M. (2009, November 29). At what cost? *The Chronicle of Higher Education.*
    Available from http://www.chroniclecareers.com/article/at-what-cost-/49253/

The original essay was published January 20, 2010, in *The Chronicle of Higher Education.*

> I've never actually known anyone who went from a
> 2-year college straight into a research institution. I'm sure
> they're out there, though, and I'll probably get e-mail
> messages from several of them.

STEPPING-STONE?

One consequence of the saturated academic market for PhDs, and the subsequent increase in their hiring at 2-year colleges, is that a growing number of applicants have come to view openings at community colleges as stepping-stones to a position at a 4-year institution. That's probably a mistake. In my experience, faculty members at 2-year colleges rarely leave to take tenure-track jobs at 4-year colleges. Moreover, such aspirations are generally pretty transparent to the easily disillusioned members of a community college search committee—a fact that could cost a candidate the job.

As I began listing the colleagues I know who have moved on to 4-year institutions, I could think of only a handful. And that, in itself, should tell you something, because I've spent 20 years working at five different community colleges in four states, as a faculty member, department chair, and dean. One reason so few people make the leap is that there aren't a lot of faculty members at 2-year colleges who actually want to leave. That may surprise you if you're one of those job seekers hungrily eyeing our market as a way to gain experience before "moving up."

Oh, sure, we all get frustrated with our jobs on occasion. And it's true—many of us who teach at 2-year colleges didn't start out with that end in mind. Like a lot of you reading this, we once pictured ourselves relaxing in the faculty lounge at some prestigious research university.

But then we took jobs at community colleges—perhaps because those were the only jobs offered, or because we fell into them, or because we too thought we would one day move up. But a funny thing happened: We learned to like working at a 2-year college. We found we enjoyed the teaching, didn't miss the emphasis on publishing, and realized we were doing something good and worthwhile by helping those students who need us most. Within a relatively short time (probably three to five years), we achieved tenure. Our salaries, though modest, at least rose steadily from year to year. We bought homes in the community and enrolled our children in the local schools. And one day we realized, a bit sadly perhaps, but mostly with relief, that we weren't going anywhere.

That's the condensed life story, I daresay, of many, and perhaps most, faculty members at 2-year colleges. Of course, some of us do try to leave, either because we have become disenchanted with the teaching load, we want to devote more time to research, or we had that plan all along. Unfortunately, very few of us succeed in moving on to the 4-year level—mostly because we can't.

A basketball coach who had been highly successful in the "junior college" ranks for many years once told me he wished he had made the move to a 4-year institution after his first or second season. By the midpoint in his career, he said, he had been definitively labeled as a "JUCO guy," and despite his winning record, no 4-year college would even consider hiring him. I think the same thing happens to most faculty members. Once we start teaching at a 2-year college, we get pigeonholed as "community college material," and most 4-year institutions don't consider people with that background as serious candidates. Part of the problem may be that we don't have the research credentials that many 4-year colleges are looking for, having spent so much of our time teaching. But mostly it's just bias on the part of the 4-year institutions. In fact, the only colleagues I've known who *have* made the jump ended up at small liberal arts colleges that also emphasize teaching over research. I've never actually known anyone who went from a 2-year college straight into a research institution. I'm sure they're out there, though, and I'll probably get e-mail messages from several of them.

The rarity of such a move makes it impractical to go into your job search with the idea of using a 2-year college as a stepping-stone. Moreover, doing so can be positively counterproductive, because search committees at community colleges will pick up on that mind-set very quickly and will almost certainly resent it. Think about it: You're implying by your attitude that what's good enough for the committee members somehow isn't good enough for you. Even if that's true, there's no way you can expect them not to be offended.

That attitude makes itself known in a number of ways: by the points you choose to dwell on in your application materials and during the interview (focusing on your dissertation topic, for instance), by the questions you ask (about time and support for research), and by your ignorance of the community college work environment, which smacks of both arrogance and laziness ("Couldn't she at least have spent a little time browsing our Web site?" committee members will ask themselves). Clearly, that kind of first impression isn't going to help you land a job at our college.

So if you really want to teach at a 4-year institution but plan to apply at 2-year colleges as well—perhaps because there are so many of them and you need a job—at least put up a good front when compiling your application materials and (if you're lucky) during the interview. Take time to learn about community colleges, our mission, our culture, our jargon. Some of my other essays might help you with that. And if, in the end, you're fortunate enough (or unfortunate enough, depending on your point of view) to get a job at a community college, there are several things you must do if you hope to move on to a 4-year campus.

First, make your move within the first three years. Remember the basketball coach I mentioned earlier? It may be true that the day you accept a job at a 2-year college, you become tainted in the minds of many faculty members and administrators at 4-year campuses. However, there's no question that the longer you stay, the more permanently affixed the community college label will be.

Second, maintain an aggressive research and publishing agenda. Every colleague I have ever known who got an interview at a 4-year college or university had a solid record of publishing scholarly articles in refereed journals. Several had books. And they accomplished all of that while teaching five courses a semester, keeping 10 office hours a week, serving on numerous committees, and advising dozens of students.

Understand that the community college will probably give you very little in terms of tangible support for your research (read: time and money). Your superiors probably won't mind that you're doing research—as long as it's on your own time. But don't expect them to be too excited that you just published a piece in the Journal of Such-and-Such or that your new book is coming out next spring.

The key phrase is "on your own time." Whatever you do in the way of research and publishing will have to be done outside the time you already put into teaching and other duties. And it will have to be done largely at your own expense. But if you ever want to teach at a 4-year institution, it's vital that you carry on with your scholarship.

Finally, don't neglect your teaching. Remember that most faculty members at 2-year colleges who make the jump end up at small liberal arts colleges that emphasize teaching. Even if you're hoping to land a job at a research university, your teaching record will still be an important factor. In fact, if you've been teaching five courses a semester for three years, that experience is probably one of the best things you've got going for you.

So devote the time and energy needed to do a good job in the classroom. Work hard to earn outstanding evaluations from department chairs, peer observers, and students. Strive to be worthy of the college's teaching awards, and talk to your chair about nominating you. The effort is bound to pay off, both during your search for a 4-year job and (meanwhile) as you move toward tenure at the 2-year college.

If you're willing to do everything I've listed—teach five courses in award-winning fashion, advise students, serve on committees, keep office hours, and oh, by the way, energetically pursue your research and publish regularly—you just might get the opportunity to step up into a tenure-track position at a 4-year college. Then again, who knows? You may already have stepped into your ideal job without even knowing it.

The original essay was published August 16, 2007, in *The Chronicle of Higher Education*.

Part 2

What Community Colleges Want

"Yes, it's true that we advertised for a Renaissance man—but we're looking for a new, <u>improved</u> Renaissance man."

> If your application packet is complete and on time, your letter well written, your résumé concise and specific—and if you're just a little bit lucky—you may very well get an interview.

APPLYING FOR JOBS AT TWO-YEAR COLLEGES

Encouraged, I hope, by my essays on teaching at community colleges, you've searched the job listings and identified the faculty positions that interest you. Perhaps the location of the campus caught your eye, or the specific job description. Maybe you have a contact there. In any case, your next objective is to land an interview. And the best way to do that is to impress the search committee with your application materials.

Perhaps I should reestablish my bona fides: I've been a faculty member for more than 23 years, at four different 2-year colleges. I've also spent 12 years as a department head. In the last decade alone, I've served on at least a dozen search committees, chairing about half of them. So I have a pretty fair idea of what it takes to get an interview.

I've also seen a lot of truly awful applications, enough to convince me that people who have spent the last five years in a research-oriented graduate-school environment often don't have the foggiest notion of how to make themselves attractive to search committees at 2-year colleges. Fortunately, it's not that difficult. It just requires a little work, an understanding of your audience, and a willingness to adapt.

The first step is to break down each ad thoroughly, paying special attention to three items: the minimum job requirements, the specific documents requested, and the application deadline. If you don't meet the minimum requirements for the job, don't apply. The committee will not consider you, so you're merely wasting its time as well as your own. If you're not sure—for example, if the ad calls for a speech degree and yours is in communication—call the academic vice president's office and ask.

Be sure to include in your packet all the necessary documents, which may include an application form, a cover letter, a résumé or CV, transcripts, and letters of reference. The list will vary from campus to campus. If you're applying for several different jobs, it's a good idea to set up a table or flow chart, listing the colleges, the various materials requested by each, and the deadlines. That way you can make sure each packet is complete and mailed on time. Human resource departments usually discard late or incomplete applications, and if they don't, the committee will.

The most important element of your packet is the cover letter. Under no circumstances should you omit this letter, which is your first opportunity to make a good impression on the search committee. Do everything in your power to portray yourself as a viable candidate who should be taken seriously, as a scholar who thinks and writes clearly, but is not in love with his or her own words, as someone who understands the mission of the 2-year college and might well be a "good fit."

The application letter should be no more than two pages long and should summarize the key information about your education, your teaching experience, and any other relevant professional activities, even if that information appears elsewhere in the packet. It should be written on a word processor and printed with an ink-jet or laser printer on good-quality paper. (Yes, I have gotten handwritten cover letters. Not a good idea.) Use a standard business letter format.

Avoid writing a terse, single-paragraph letter that merely refers to your attached CV. Such letters tell the committee very little about the writer other than that he or she is probably lazy and perhaps arrogant as well. Some applicants seem to believe their wonderful CV will speak for itself. It won't. The committee wants to know more about you than that: how you communicate, what you think is the most important of your qualifications, your attitude toward the job as apparent in the tone of your letter.

Address your letter to an actual individual, not just to some faceless, generic entity, such as "Search Committee" or "Office of Human Resources." If the ad doesn't name an individual, take a few moments to look up the name of the college's director of human resources on the Internet. The ad may direct you to address your application packet in a certain way—such as "Attention: History Search Committee"—and by all means do that. But you should still try to find out the name of the faculty member leading the committee (a phone call or two should be sufficient) and address your cover letter to him or her.

The body of the letter will vary somewhat depending on the institution and the exact job for which you're applying. Don't send a form letter to every college on your list. Take the time to customize each letter, tailoring it specifically to fit the job description and the institution. Mention the college by name. The committee members will be impressed that you're applying for their job, not just for a job.

In your opening paragraph, identify the specific job for which you are applying and tell where you saw it advertised. Then, in a paragraph or two, emphasize your primary claims on the job, i.e., your experience and your education. If you have teaching experience beyond being a TA—and especially if you have experience at 2-year colleges—be sure to feature that prominently. If not, lead with your academic qualifications and play up whatever experience you do have. List some specific courses you've taught. You're trying here to convey the impression of someone for whom teaching has been a central activity.

In a few sentences about your education, mention not only your degrees and where you earned them, but also name some specific courses that you've taken, especially those that relate to the job in question. Whether or not you're minimally qualified has already been determined before the committee members read your letter. Now they want to know whether your education has been relevant and whether it makes you a good fit for their institution.

Next take a paragraph or two to mention any other professional accomplishments: your dissertation, conferences you've attended, publications and presentations, memberships, awards. These items have the potential to impress the committee and perhaps even set you apart from other candidates. But don't dwell on them; that will make it seem as though you're really looking for a research job. Whatever you do, don't spend the bulk of your letter synopsizing your dissertation or regaling the committee members with details of your latest research project. They'll simply wonder, "Why is this person applying here?" Conclude your letter by thanking the reader for his or her time, stating your availability (be as available as possible), and asking for an interview. ("May I come to Centerville to discuss this position with you in person?") Hey, it doesn't hurt to ask.

The second most important document in your application packet is the résumé. Note that I've referred to this as a CV above; that's because graduate students are accustomed to thinking in those terms. When you're applying to a 2-year college, however, you should use a résumé instead—the difference being that a CV is a detailed account of your academic career whereas a résumé merely hits the high points.

There are scores of résumé formats available online and in various textbooks. For your purposes, any decent format that employs a good balance between print and white space will do. The main thing is to put the most important information—your education and teaching experience—right up front. In the experience section, be very specific about what you've accomplished: what courses you've taught, what your other responsibilities were, what additional tasks you took on. Then you can list your other professional achievements separately, under such headings as "Publications and Presentations." Here again, don't go into too much detail. The fact that you have a few things under each category will work in your favor, but overemphasizing your research and scholarship at this stage might cause the committee to question your suitability.

Finally, be sure to list references, including detailed contact information, at the end of your résumé—even if the ad doesn't ask you to. Those references should be current, people who know you well and who can address your teaching abilities. A professor who observed you in the classroom, for example, makes a better reference than one who supervised your dissertation.

If your application packet is complete and on time, your letter well written, your résumé concise and specific—and if you're just a little bit lucky—you may very well get an interview. And that's why you'll want to be sure to read my essays in the next section on how to surmount that last and most daunting barrier. Meanwhile, good luck with your applications.

The original essay was published December 12, 2003, in *The Chronicle of Higher Education.*

> Your objective as an applicant . . . like a character in some
> sort of fantasy role-playing game, is to make it past
> each of those watchers: the HR clerk, the search
> committee chair, and the committee members.

HOW TO MAKE YOUR APPLICATION STAND OUT

In preparing composition students for our state's writing proficiency exam, I always begin by explaining how their work will be evaluated. I've found that knowing what raters are looking for helps students better understand how to prepare their essays. I'd like to apply that same approach to another sort of proficiency exam: the job application. Having served on many search committees at 2-year colleges, I have a pretty good idea how applications are evaluated. My objective is to help you understand the process, too, so you can craft your documents accordingly.

The first thing you should know is what happens to your application once it arrives. At most 2-year colleges, job applications go directly to the human resources office, rather than to a dean, department chair, or search committee chair. An HR clerk logs and files them by position but usually doesn't make any other judgments about them, except perhaps to note if they're complete. Some HR departments let applicants know if something's missing, but others simply file the application as is, or discard it.

When I chair a search committee, my second priority (after hiring the best people) is operating efficiently, which means not taking up any more of my colleagues' time than necessary. I try to streamline at least the first part of the process by eliminating, early on, any applications that don't strictly meet the stated requirements. If an application doesn't contain all the materials we requested in the ad, I toss it. (OK, I don't literally throw it away, but I do relegate it to the "incomplete" pile, which means it won't be considered.) If an applicant isn't actually qualified for the position—doesn't hold the relevant degree, doesn't have enough credit hours teaching in the field, doesn't have the required experience—I toss that person's file, too.

What happens next depends on the number of applications. Essentially, each committee member is trying to narrow down the number of applicants whom we'll talk about when we meet. With just a few, we'll discuss all of them. But if there's really a large number—I've had as many as 175 for an English position—it helps for each member to identify, say, a top 10. Given natural differences of opinion among committee members, that means we'll probably end up discussing 30 or 40 applications and trying to narrow that pool down to the 8 or 10 people we'll invite for interviews.

Your objective as an applicant, then, like a character in some sort of fantasy role-playing game, is to make it past each of those watchers: the HR clerk, the search committee chair, and the committee members. That means, first of all, that your application *must* arrive by the stated deadline. If it doesn't, HR will most likely not even file it with the others, and the search committee will never even see it.

Second, your application must be complete. Read the job ad carefully, then read it again. Include *exactly* the documents requested. Does the ad call for a CV or a résumé? (There is a difference, and examples of both are available in numerous reference books.) Does it ask for actual reference letters or just a list of references? Does it specify official transcripts or just copies? How about a statement of teaching philosophy? If you don't understand what the ad is looking for, call the college's HR office and ask. But don't just leave something out.

Third, make sure you're actually qualified for the job. If the job ad asks for "a master's degree with 18 graduate semester hours in accounting," that's what the committee wants. Perhaps, with a master's in mathematics and three or four accounting classes under your belt, you could easily teach the introductory courses offered at a 2-year college, but that's irrelevant. If you don't meet at least the minimum requirements stated in the ad, you won't be considered.

My advice up to this point has been pretty basic. But trust me: If you follow it, your application is already looking better than many. There's a good chance you're now in the "to be considered" pool. To take the next step into the "to be invited for an interview" pool, there's one more thing you need to do: Write a killer letter of application. I say "letter of application" because it should be precisely that, and not just a brief "cover letter" noting what's contained in the rest of your application. This letter is your opportunity to set yourself apart from other applicants who meet the basic requirements. Your letter must be long enough to contain real substance but not so long that it becomes irritating. Write at least a page, single-spaced, but no more than a page and a half.

Your letter should also be professionally produced, using a decent printer, good-quality paper, and a standard business letter format (again, available in numerous references). The grammar, spelling, and punctuation must be perfect and the writing clear and engaging. In terms of content, the letter should begin by identifying the specific job you are seeking and naming the college. (Yes, that means writing a separate letter for each job—something you should always do, anyway.) End the first paragraph by stating that you believe yourself to be a strong candidate and hope to be given serious consideration.

Use the next two or three paragraphs to expand upon your claims to the job—namely, your academic credentials and teaching experience. Even if you don't have a great deal of teaching experience, spend some time talking about the experience you do have. We want to know that you actually enjoy teaching and that you have some idea what you're getting yourself into on our campus.

If you have a doctorate, that's great, but don't spend more than two or three sentences discussing your dissertation. By all means, let us know you wrote one (that's still impressive) and tell us what it has to do with your teaching, if anything. But no lengthy exegeses, please. Once you've covered those important areas, you can add a paragraph detailing any other relevant accomplishments, such as teaching awards, publications, and involvement in professional groups. Conclude by referencing your CV or résumé and asking for an interview.

As a serial committee member, I can tell you that if you do all of those things, your application will definitely wind up in my "to be discussed" pile. And that's right where you want it to be.

The original essay was published November 23, 2009, in *The Chronicle of Higher Education.*

> Pick up two master's degrees because you like the subjects, not because a school is more likely to hire you. How happy will you be teaching chemistry if you really don't like it? Will you be any good for your students?

ARE TWO MASTERS BETTER THAN ONE?

s it an advantage on the community college job market to be qualified to teach in two fields? As someone who writes and speaks frequently on the topic of 2-year college academic careers, I'm often asked that question by aspiring faculty members. "I am working on a master's in international relations," wrote one, noting that the program will meet the minimum of 18 credits that most 2-year colleges require to teach political science at the undergraduate level. "I enjoy history," the writer continued, "and am considering taking the extra classes to reach the 18 credits in history too. Do community colleges want someone who can teach in two separate social-science departments?" The answer: It may depend on where you're applying, and on whether the two areas in which you teach are housed together.

I've been involved in faculty searches at four 2-year colleges—two of them small and rural, the other two large and urban or suburban. At the smaller colleges, we certainly did have an interest in hiring people who could "wear more than one hat." In fact, at one of them, we routinely advertised for faculty members who could teach in two related disciplines, such as English and speech.

However, I can't remember either of the larger colleges ever placing such an ad. Nor was I ever told, as a member or chairman of search committees, that we should specifically look for someone who could teach in a second discipline. In fact, I personally know only a handful of full-time faculty members at my current college (a large, multi-campus, metropolitan institution) who actively teach in more than one discipline. That's just my institutional memory, of course, but I can see a few practical reasons for the difference. Depending on how small the college is, there may be a financial need for one person to teach in more than one discipline. In certain disciplines, where only a few sections are offered each term, the only way to get a qualified full-time person may be to hire someone who can also teach in a more "popular" discipline.

Rather than rely solely on my impressions, however, I conducted an informal survey of colleagues at my own and other 2-year institutions. Chris, a science professor at a small, rural college who teaches physics and chemistry, notes that his institution has hired "some rare combinations." "Do you realize," he asks, "how hard it is to find someone with at least 18 hours in both business and accounting? How about sociology and criminal justice? But we have only 21 full-time faculty members. And only two sections of accounting each term, and only one class of criminal-justice students for those courses that we teach each term." Ray, who has taught and held various administrative positions at a number of 2-year colleges and is currently chairman of a social science department, believes "it would be to an applicant's advantage to be qualified in a second area," especially in something like anthropology or geography. In those disciplines, he says, there are rarely "enough sections to justify a full-time tenure-track position."

I did find some exceptions to the general rule that large, urban colleges shy away from such dual hires. Frank, chairman of a humanities department at a large suburban campus, says his college often hires instructors to teach in more than one area: "I would say definitely yes, that certification in two related fields makes people more attractive for tenure-track work." He has faculty members who teach reading and English (one of the more frequent combinations), film and speech, English and speech, and English and ESL. He also hopes to hire, in the near future, he says, people who can teach English and theater, English and journalism, and religion and philosophy.

An important caveat, however, comes from another colleague—Don, a former professor and chairman of a science department who is now an academic dean: "The problem with a candidate having two teaching fields is that they must be similar enough to fall under the same department. It is unfortunate, but most colleges are so departmentalized that it is rare to see two departments share a person."

It's worth noting that all of the disciplinary combinations I've mentioned— physics and chemistry, geography and anthropology, English and speech—meet that criterion. But job candidates shouldn't make the mistake of thinking that departments at community colleges are as rigidly separated as they are at many 4-year institutions. The reader who sent the original question described political science and history as "two separate social science departments." What that correspondent may not understand—and the same goes for many first-time applicants—is that departments at 2-year colleges are almost always broadly based groupings of related disciplines. Rather than a bunch of separate programs, we have departments of humanities, which might include English, speech, philosophy, and religion; departments of social sciences (psychology, sociology, history, political science); and science departments (biology, chemistry, physics).

On a practical level, what that means for faculty members is that the chairman who schedules and assigns the staffing for physics classes is probably doing the same for chemistry. It's just common sense to assume that that person might appreciate the flexibility inherent in being able to use the same faculty member in more than one subdiscipline—especially at small colleges where, without that flexibility, some sections might go uncovered or be taught only by adjuncts.

The same advantage, however, does not apply when the faculty member teaches in two areas that aren't closely related or housed together—English and history, for example. In that case, a faculty member's desire to teach in both areas at a community college could create conflict between the department heads, who might be unwilling to let courses in their own area go unstaffed in order to share a faculty member who also wants to teach in another department.

A related question that I have also heard from some readers: Is it better for a job seeker at 2-year colleges to have a PhD in one field, or two master's degrees in different but related fields? My ad hoc panel of experts was somewhat divided on that. Mariam, chairwoman of a large science department, says her urban college would probably prefer the PhD, but she thinks "that most 2-year colleges would rather have someone who is qualified in multiple areas."

Don, the academic dean, believes that "having the doctorate in the field gives one a better chance at getting an interview than does having a second teaching field," but he is quick to point out that the higher degree isn't necessarily an advantage during the interview, where what often counts most is who performs better before the hiring committee. He recalls one search where an applicant with a PhD did very poorly during the interview and a candidate fresh from a master's program "gave a great interview. The better interviewee got the job."

Perhaps the best advice comes from Chris, the science professor at a rural college, who warns, "Graduate school for the sake of employability is always a bad idea. Get a PhD because you want to, not because it is the ticket to your dream job. Pick up two master's degrees because you like the subjects, not because a school is more likely to hire you. How happy will you be teaching chemistry if you really don't like it? Will you be any good for your students?"

In the end, you must remember why you chose the community college sector: You want to teach. Moreover, you chose your graduate major because you thought you would enjoy teaching that subject. If there's more than one subject that interests you, by all means, take enough graduate courses to be qualified to teach in that area, too. Having the second field may or may not help you get a job, but it could help make your job more fulfilling once you get one.

The original essay was published January 14, 2005, in *The Chronicle of Higher Education.*

Because of the 18-hours-in-the-discipline requirement, we have medical doctors who "aren't qualified" to teach anatomy and physiology, coaches who can't teach physical education courses, and professional actors who are not allowed to teach theater.

SOLVING THE CREDENTIALS PUZZLE

Much of my e-mail comes from people thinking about going on the community college job market—or going on it again, if the current year's round of hiring has just about ended. Their questions often have to do with the issue of credentials: Am I qualified to teach such-and-such at a 2-year college? Is a degree in X better than a degree in Y? Do I need more graduate hours in Z? I answer those e-mail messages personally, but I believe the correspondents represent a large number of job seekers who are equally confused about the credentials they need to teach at a community college but are not sure where to turn.

For example, one woman wrote to ask the following: "My PhD is in neuropharmacology. Most of my course work has titles like 'Advanced Pharmacology' or 'Receptor Biochemistry,' which don't seem to be a neat fit for either a biology or a chemistry position. I've been hired as a full-time person in both biology and chemistry departments at several [4-year] schools in [a Southern state]. I'm assuming that I'm SACS-qualified to teach [at a 2-year college] in both these disciplines."

Well, maybe—and maybe not. Before I proceed, let me explain that SACS refers to the Southern Association of Colleges and Schools, the regional accrediting body for the vast majority of higher education institutions in the South, where I live. Each region of the country has its accreditor: the New England Association of Schools and Colleges, the North Central Association of Colleges and Schools, the Northwest Commission on Colleges and Universities, and so on. Because all of those organizations have similar criteria, what I'm about to say should apply to most people (although the specifics may vary).

Turning back to the issues raised in the letter, the fact that several Southern colleges have hired my correspondent in the past doesn't necessarily mean she is SACS-qualified to teach at a 2-year college. Some institutions pay closer attention to accreditation guidelines than others, and 4-year programs often have different rules.

Generally speaking, to teach in programs that award associate of arts or associate of science degrees—i.e., to teach at a community college—faculty members are required by accreditors to have at least a master's degree *and* a minimum of 18 graduate credit hours in the subject they are teaching. Read that statement again carefully and note the wording: While you need a master's, you are not required to have one in the specific subject you are teaching; you are required to have completed 18 graduate credit hours in that subject. And even if you do have a degree in the subject you hope to teach, that degree must have included 18 credit hours *in that subject* in order for you to be allowed to teach it at a 2-year college.

The e-mail message above provides a perfect case in point. The writer has a PhD in neuropharmacology and no doubt took graduate courses related to biology and chemistry. But the true test of whether she will be able to teach biology or chemistry at the 2-year college level is not the doctorate itself, but rather if it included enough courses specifically in biology and chemistry. Simply put, in order to teach biology, she must have earned 18 graduate semester hours in biology. To teach chemistry, she'll need 18 hours of chemistry credits. Without those hours, her PhD is irrelevant. It would only become relevant if she were applying to teach courses in neuropharmacology. Sounds a little nuts, I know.

Department heads and academic deans at 2-year colleges deal with this sort of apparent contradiction every day. Because of the 18-hours-in-the-discipline requirement, we have medical doctors who "aren't qualified" to teach anatomy and physiology, coaches who can't teach physical education courses, and professional actors who are not allowed to teach theater. That can be frustrating for administrators but even more so, I know, for applicants.

Two other fields in which the 18-hour requirement often creates havoc are business and education. With recent fluctuations in the economy, 2-year colleges are seeing a number of MBAs applying to teach full or part time. Once again, the problem is that, in most cases, their degree programs include course work in many different disciplines—9 hours in marketing courses, 6 in accounting, 12 in management, and so on. No doubt the intent is to produce a broad base of business knowledge. But as beneficial as such a degree might be in the private sector, it poses problems for someone seeking a teaching position at a 2-year college. If a community college doesn't offer upper-level business courses, what can an MBA teach there? Very often the answer is "nothing," unless he or she happens to have 18 credit hours in a specific discipline such as accounting.

Education degrees can put job seekers in a similar fix. Of course, many 2-year colleges do offer education courses, which can be taught by applicants with master's degrees in education. But often we'll get an application from someone with a degree in English education, for instance, seeking a faculty position in English. The question becomes, how many graduate hours in English did that candidate actually complete? How many of the courses had an "EDUC" prefix, rather than an "ENGL" one? At that point, the transcript review process can become even more confusing. Some 2-year colleges, in evaluating whether applicants have enough credit hours in the field in which they want to teach, will allow only courses with ENGL prefixes to be considered. By contrast, other colleges might allow courses with education prefixes to be counted if they use words like "language," "literature," or "composition" in the course titles.

As a department head, I frequently argued for such "exceptions," often submitting catalog course descriptions in support of a candidate. Which brings us back to our e-mail correspondent. Is she qualified to teach biology or chemistry at a 2-year college? Now you know the answer: It depends on how many of her graduate courses had "BIOL" or "CHEM" prefixes—or on the number of pharmacology courses for which a supportive department head or dean could make a case that they should be counted as biology or chemistry courses.

And what if the candidate just doesn't have the hours? Say her transcript has been thoroughly evaluated, the department head has made a good pitch to hire her, but she's still been turned down for a biology teaching position because she doesn't have 18 hours in biology. Then what? If she wants to teach at a 2-year college, she will have to go back to graduate school and pick up the additional credit hours she needs. After all, she might be only two or three courses short; she needn't begin a new degree program. Then she should apply again, highlighting the fact that, along with her PhD in neuropharmacology, she does indeed have 18 graduate semester hours in biology (or chemistry, or whatever). I think most committees would find her a fairly attractive candidate.

So if you're thinking about going on the 2-year market next year, you might want to double-check your transcript to make sure you're qualified (according to the accrediting agencies) for the position you want. And if you were turned down for jobs this year because you weren't qualified, consider going back to graduate school. That way, during the next round of hiring, your application will find its way into the "qualified" pile from which the eventual interviewees will be chosen. That's still no guarantee you'll get an interview, but if your application is tossed onto the "not qualified" pile, I can guarantee you won't.

The original essay was published June 20, 2008, in *The Chronicle of Higher Education.*

> As a practical matter ... those who want to pursue faculty careers at 2-year colleges are most likely to be successful if ... they make sure they have at least a master's degree with a minimum of 18 graduate-semester hours in the teaching discipline.

GUIDELINES VS. REQUIREMENTS

Some regional accrediting agencies have relaxed their standards for faculty credentials at 2-year colleges—or have they? What's the difference between a guideline and a requirement? Not much, if the "guideline" is enforced like a requirement.

Yet that semantic distinction was the subject of several e-mail messages and phone calls I received in response to my essay on teaching credentials at community colleges. One of those calls came from Belle Wheelan, president of the Southern Association of Colleges and Schools (SACS) Commission on Colleges (personal communication, June, 2008). Wheelan took issue with my characterization of SACS's "guidelines" [SACS, 2006] (her word) as "requirements" (my word)—specifically, the so-called 18-hour rule. Here's the key passage from the essay in question: "Generally speaking, to teach in programs that award associate of arts or associate of science degrees—i.e., to teach at a community college—faculty members are required by accreditors to have at least a master's degree *and* a minimum of 18 graduate credit hours in the subject they are teaching." According to Wheelan, "that's just not true." In 2002, she said, the regional accrediting agency abandoned the 80 or so "must" statements it had previously used to assess institutional compliance in favor of about 40 broad-based "principles."

"Of course, institutions can still use the 18-hour rule if they want to, but they're no longer required to do so," she told me. She went on to say that SACS, like other accrediting agencies around the country, has relaxed its standards for evaluating faculty credentials. "If you have a banker, for instance, who doesn't necessarily have the academic credentials but has successfully run a business for 20 years, an institution could probably make a good case to justify that person's teaching an intro-to-business course," Wheelan said.

Obviously, that sort of flexibility would represent a welcome change from the way SACS and other accreditors have done business in the past. Because the case Wheelan describes involving the banker is exactly the kind of situation I dealt with repeatedly when I was a department chairman: people who were clearly qualified to teach specific courses by any rational definition of the word but who could not be certified and hired because they did not meet the strict academic requirements for the job. Of course, I was a chairman before the reforms Wheelan mentioned, or at least before word of those reforms filtered down to the campuses. So I'm not by any means questioning the literal veracity of her statements. Nor do I have a death-wish-like desire to antagonize SACS—the organization that accredits my own institution, which has another review coming up in 2011.

But in the interests of my readers, who are grappling with very practical questions like "Am I qualified to teach X at community college Y?" I have to point out a few problems with her distinction between requirements and guidelines. The first is that, whatever the accreditors may say, people at 2-year colleges nationally are still dealing with confusing and seemingly contradictory credentials problems. Many of them e-mailed their horror stories to me about being denied the opportunity to teach at a 2-year college because they were judged unqualified—based on the 18-hour rule and other such "guidelines."

One correspondent, for instance, has been unable to get a job teaching statistics at community colleges in his home state because college administrators—and by extension, he assumes, the regional accrediting agency (not SACS)—require faculty members in a math department to have a degree in mathematics. At most 2-year colleges, statistics courses are taught in the math department and have a "MAT" prefix. Unfortunately for the job candidate, all the courses in his PhD program in statistics had "STAT" prefixes. So, under the 18-hour guideline, he has been deemed unqualified to teach in a community college math department. Another correspondent is pursuing a degree in teaching English to speakers of other languages but has been told she can't teach freshman composition courses.

Perhaps the reason for such mindless nitpicking is simply, as Wheelan suggested, that news of the new, more flexible guidelines hasn't gotten out. Or maybe the problem is that, while the standards themselves have become more flexible, the people applying them—administrators and site-visit team members—haven't. (Note: The "site-visit team" is a group of faculty members and administrators from other institutions assigned by an accrediting agency to review an institution's accreditation.)

In the case of SACS, the new guidelines, although welcome, still seem sufficiently open to interpretation to create confusion among job applicants as well as disparity among institutions. Here's the revised statement on credentials for faculty members at 2-year colleges, taken from the SACS Web site and dated December 2006: "Institutions should use the following as credential guidelines … Faculty teaching associate degree courses designed for transfer to a baccalaureate degree: doctorate or master's degree in the teaching discipline or master's degree with a concentration in the teaching discipline (a minimum of 18 graduate semester hours in the teaching discipline)." Honestly, how much difference do you see between that language and what I wrote in my last column?

Another potential problem is evident in Wheelan's example of the banker who might be able to teach business courses. Remember how she put it? An institution "could probably make a good case to justify that person's teaching." In other words, if a candidate does not meet the credential guidelines cited above—essentially, still the 18-hour rule—then the onus is on the institution to justify hiring that person.

That's fine, so long as the college has both gutsy department chairs who will argue for unorthodox candidates and open-minded administrators who will see the logic in those arguments. Realistically, though, how many institutions does that last sentence describe? More to the point, how many colleges will go to the trouble of trying to make a case for someone who doesn't exactly fit the profile, especially if other candidates do?

The truth is, some 2-year colleges might hire that banker as an adjunct if they just need someone to teach an intro-to-business course. But very few would hire him or her full time, much less on the tenure track. As a practical matter, then, those who want to pursue faculty careers at 2-year colleges are most likely to be successful if—as I said in my original essay—they make sure they have at least a master's degree with a minimum of 18 graduate semester hours in the teaching discipline. (A few minutes spent perusing the job listings in *The Chronicle* for positions at community colleges will, I think, bear out that conclusion.)

In all fairness, SACS and other regional accrediting agencies deserve credit for their attempts to streamline, liberalize, and demystify the credentialing process. More power to Wheelan, in particular, who described herself as a "one-woman crusade to get the word out" about her organization's more-flexible new guidelines. Let's hope she's successful, and that administrators as well as those reviewing credentials get the memo. Until then, prospective faculty members at 2-year colleges can save themselves a lot of headaches by interpreting "guideline" as "requirement."

References

Southern Association of Colleges and Schools. (2006, December). *Faculty credentials: Guidelines.* Decatur, GA: Author. Available from http://www.sacscoc. org/pdf/081705/faculty%20credentials.pdf

The original essay was published August 7, 2008, in *The Chronicle of Higher Education*.

> If you are thinking about applying to community colleges, or have already done so, you probably want to know what you're up against. Based on my experience, I think search committees are seeking five characteristics. . .

WHAT COMMUNITY COLLEGES WANT

L et me follow up my ambitious title with a disclaimer: I don't pretend to speak for every 2-year college in America, nor do I claim to know exactly what all 1,195 of them are looking for in a faculty member. On the other hand, I have spent my entire career at community colleges—23 years, to be exact, at five different institutions in four states. I've been a part-time faculty member, a full-time faculty member, a program director, a department head, and a dean. I've served on at least a dozen faculty search committees (honestly, I've lost track), chairing about half of them. And I've been a regular contributor to "The Two-Year Track" advice column in *The Chronicle* for almost seven years now.

So I think I have a pretty fair idea of what 2-year colleges are looking for when they conduct a faculty search, as many are doing right now. And if you are thinking about applying to community colleges, or have already done so, you probably want to know what you're up against. Based on my experience, I think search committees are seeking five characteristics, two of which I'll cover in this essay, and the other three in the next one.

First and foremost, search committees are looking for candidates who are *clearly* qualified for the position advertised. If you're not clearly qualified—in a way that is both well documented and easy to demonstrate—the committee probably won't even consider you. I've actually heard candidates say, when deciding whether to apply for a particular teaching position, "Well, I might not exactly meet the requirements, but I think I'll throw my hat in the ring, anyway." And they honestly think the search committee will somehow see that they're perfect for the job, or at least they believe they can make a good argument in their cover letter.

That's not going to work. The first step in any search process is to weed out those applicants who don't meet the minimum qualifications so committee members won't have to waste any more time than necessary reviewing the files. If that sounds harsh, consider this: The last time I chaired a search committee in English, we received 174 applications. As chair, I conducted the first review and was able to eliminate about 25 people who weren't qualified, based on the original job ad. Then the rest of the committee members only had to look at 150 files, saving a fair amount of grief and wasted time.

Being clearly qualified to teach at a 2-year college means that you meet the specified degree and credit-hour requirements. Usually you must have, at minimum, a master's degree and 18 graduate semester hours in the teaching discipline. And you must have the transcripts to prove it. Your degree must be in the field specified unless the ad expressly stipulates "or related field." You might think, for instance, that your master's in psychology qualifies you to teach first- and second-year sociology courses, and you may, in fact, be more than able to teach those courses. But don't expect search committee members to reach the same conclusion, or even to give the matter much thought. If the ad calls for a sociology instructor, the committee is almost certainly looking for someone with a degree in sociology.

The exceptions to that rule: Committees intent on hiring a particular candidate—a loyal, long-term adjunct or an administrator's nephew—may be willing to overlook certain requirements. In addition, committees hiring in disciplines in which they must compete for good candidates might also make exceptions, as might small colleges that need someone who can teach in more than one field.

Being qualified also means proving that you have the necessary years of experience. Most job ads call for at least a year of teaching experience, some for two or three. Some specify "full-time experience," but many don't. A few even provide a formula for equating part-time experience to full-time—a certain number of courses equals a year's worth of teaching. This is one area you might be able to fudge a bit, but you have to be close. Search committee members aren't stupid (contrary to what you might think in a few months, after you've received a rejection letter or two). The bottom line: If you clearly fall short in either area—credit hours in the discipline or amount of experience—you probably won't be able to talk your way around that deficiency in a cover letter (although many try). Better to wait until you *are* qualified, then apply.

After determining who meets the minimum requirements and who doesn't, the next thing search committees look for in reviewing the applicants is good teachers. Very good teachers. Because, as has been discussed ad infinitum in a variety of forums, including this one, teaching is what a faculty career at a community college is all about. How can search committees determine whether someone is a good teacher simply by looking at an application? The answer is that they can't always. But every candidate's file contains a number of textual clues.

The obvious indicator—years of teaching experience—is, perhaps, not the most important one. Those of us on search committees also look at the institutions where a candidate has taught—community college experience is always a plus—and even at the types of courses listed. Perhaps most telling is the emphasis that applicants place on teaching in their cover letters. Letters in which candidates give lengthy (and often tedious) summaries of their theses or dissertations are not uncommon. Letters in which the writers speak glowingly of their teaching experiences and accomplishments in the classroom are much rarer. On this issue I can safely say I'm speaking for all 1,195 community colleges: We want the best teachers we can find.

What else are community colleges looking for in a faculty member? I'll talk about that in the next essay, but here's a glimpse: We want candidates who understand and embrace the community college mission, who are worker bees, and who are good colleagues.

The original essay was published October 14, 2008, in *The Chronicle of Higher Education.*

> The best applicants seem to embrace the fundamental truth of community college teaching—that our job . . . is to serve all students to the best of our ability, to challenge the gifted just as they would be challenged at a university, and to enable the underprepared . . . to attain the same level.

WHAT COMMUNITY COLLEGES WANT, PART 2

When those of us at 2-year colleges go looking for new faculty members, we first seek applicants who fit the job requirements and who are top-notch teachers (see "What Community Colleges Want"). But that's not all we're looking for in a new hire. In this essay, I'd like to focus on three additional characteristics we seek in a faculty candidate: an understanding of the community college mission, a willingness to work that extends beyond the classroom, and a healthy respect for collegiality.

Speaking as someone who has served on more than a few search committees, I would have to say the main problem with most applicants is that they seem to have no idea what a community college is all about. That ignorance can manifest itself in the candidate's application materials—for instance, a cover letter written for a job at a research university—and again during the interview process. Nothing turns off our hiring committees like a candidate who is obviously looking for a research job but has applied to one or two community colleges as a fallback position. And yes, we can tell. Usually your cover letter is long and generic, doesn't mention our college at all (or only briefly at the beginning), and waxes verbose about your research agenda.

It's even more obvious when such candidates make it to the campus interview, where they are peppered with questions about their teaching philosophy, their views on developmental education, and their experience with diverse student populations. Suddenly, the ill-prepared applicant begins to sound like a shady politician under the lights, trying desperately to change the subject: "Um, did I mention that I was a research assistant for Professor So-and-So?"

The best applicants—the ones whose files make it into the "definitely interview" pile and who continue to impress in person—know exactly what they're getting into in seeking the job. They've done their research, not only on our campus but on community colleges in general. They realize that most 2-year colleges have open-door policies, admitting basically anyone with a high school diploma or the equivalent. They understand that, while they may well teach some students with SAT scores of 1950, they will also have students sitting in those same classrooms who never took the college boards and wouldn't have scored high if they had.

Most important, the best applicants seem to embrace the fundamental truth of community college teaching—that our job as faculty members is to serve all students to the best of our ability, to challenge the gifted just as they would be challenged at a university, and to enable the underprepared, as much as humanly possible, to attain the same level. That's why someone whose cover letter devotes three paragraphs to a detailed exegesis of a dissertation, but not a single paragraph to teaching, doesn't interest us.

Another quality that search committees look for is a willingness to jump right into the life of the institution beyond the classroom and share in the myriad tasks that go hand in hand with teaching at a community college. It's doubtful that someone who's never taught at a 2-year college can fully understand the amount of grunt work involved: the countless committees to be staffed, student organizations to be sponsored, departmental exams to be scored, adjunct faculty members to be supervised. So the need to find worker bees is partly institutional: Our colleges need people who are willing to help out. Otherwise, important things won't get done.

But our interest is also personal. By the time we sit on a search committee, most of us have been at a community college for years, perhaps even decades. Year after year, we have done all the grunt work. Quite frankly, we're looking for someone to take on some of those responsibilities and perhaps give us a much-needed break. We don't expect applicants, especially those fresh from graduate programs, to have experience in all of those areas. But candidates who have *some* experience—who have worked with an undergraduate organization or taken on some departmental duties in graduate school, for instance—and who, beyond that, demonstrate in their cover letter a willingness to pitch in, well, those are the people we want to talk to.

Finally, the experienced faculty members who make up the search committee are looking, individually and collectively, for good colleagues. We want people who will not only help shoulder some of the burden but who plan on staying, and around whom we will be comfortable for years to come. We're not necessarily looking for friends or allies, but we also aren't interested in sharing the copy room for the next 10 years with a whiner, a prima donna (or, as one of my freshman-comp students once wrote, a "pre-Madonna"), or someone who's clearly high maintenance.

If you're thinking that the last criterion turns the whole hiring process into a bit of a popularity contest, you're right—to an extent. Professors at 2-year colleges are like any other academics. Assuming candidates' qualifications and experience are roughly equal, we want to interview those whose application materials make the best impression, and hire those we like the best during the interview. You may also think that this is the point at which academic politics enter into the equation and you're right about that, too—but, again, only to an extent.

On the one hand, what Kissinger famously said about university politics—that they're so vicious because the stakes are so low—certainly holds true to some degree for community colleges. On the other hand, because academic departments at 2-year colleges don't incorporate nearly as many subspecialties, we don't usually have the kinds of sharp ideological and intellectual divisions frequently found at 4-year institutions. That said, it's still possible for a job candidate to "step in it" during an interview (or even in a cover letter), effectively alienating one side or the other in a longstanding internal debate (process or product? Western canon or world cultures?).

The best candidates avoid such pitfalls by staying away from politically or emotionally charged issues in their application materials, focusing instead on academic preparation, teaching experience, and other pertinent information. They also, even if they're not Dale Carnegie graduates, manage to come across in their interviews as cordial, likeable, humble—basically, people that other professionals would want to work with. Surprisingly, some candidates don't even make an effort to present themselves that way.

The successful applicants recognize what it takes to land a tenure-track job at a community college. They've made sure they're well qualified before applying and learned how to emphasize their teaching experience. They also understand and embrace the community college mission, display a willingness to roll up their sleeves and get to work, and practice good people skills. And that's why they get hired. Contrary to popular mythology, it's rarely just dumb luck.

The original essay was published November 17, 2008, in *The Chronicle of Higher Education*.

At 4-year institutions, departments may well turn up their noses at hiring their own adjuncts. But the fact is, at community colleges, adjuncts have certain built-in advantages when they apply for full-time positions.

WHY ADJUNCTS HAVE AN EDGE (EXCEPT WHEN THEY DON'T)

Every hiring season, I'm sure to hear from representatives of two groups: those who believe the search process at community colleges is biased in favor of adjuncts (or "internal candidates") and those adjuncts who are angry because they didn't get a full-time job. Consider the e-mail I received from "Keith," who insisted that "community colleges are not looking for the best teachers. Most committees are looking to advance their own sociopolitical agendas and/or simply will hire a person who has been an adjunct in the department for a number of years. They are more interested in seniority than quality."

Compare that with a letter to the editor written by Betsy Smith, an adjunct professor at Cape Cod Community College, in response to my essay, "What Community Colleges Want, Part 2." Smith wrote: "Why doesn't Rob Jenkins hire some of the adjuncts he's forced to supervise instead of interviewing new PhDs who want to be working at research universities? If he looked among his contingent faculty, he would find qualified candidates galore—smart, experienced, and often highly degreed teachers well acquainted with the mission of the college and probably desperate for the benefits and job security that a full-time tenure-track appointment would bring."

Her complaint echoes the ones I heard every spring while I served as department chairman and campus academic dean. Long-term adjunct instructors would come by my office to ask why they hadn't gotten a full-time job (again), to hurl invective, or to quit. In directing their anger at me, they made the same mistake as Betsy, assuming that as an administrator I controlled who we interviewed and eventually hired.

Actually, I had no more say in those decisions than any other member of the search committee, even when I chaired it. Some years I wasn't even on the committee. But I understood the disappointment and the need, like displaced Okies in *The Grapes of Wrath,* to take their frustration out personally on someone. I just happened to be that someone. It comes as no surprise, then, that both Keith and Betsy seem to perceive sinister motives on the part of those doing the hiring. Keith believes committees are merely "looking to advance their own ... agendas," while Betsy writes of the adjuncts I was "forced to supervise," as if I found that part of my job somehow distasteful. (I didn't.)

So which of them is right? Is there some sort of conspiracy among tenured faculty members to keep out anyone who isn't already on the inside? Or do blind and insensitive administrators refuse to recognize the talent right under their noses? The answer is that both accusations are probably true—in certain instances. But most of the time, neither one is true. Two-year colleges are looking for the best-qualified teachers they can find, whether they come from inside the college or from someplace else.

Sure, some committee members may have their own personal agendas, wanting to hire adjuncts they've been mentors to, or those they've become close friends with. But based on my experience, at least, Keith's charge that all committee members are cynically self-interested, or even that they're somehow in cahoots, doesn't ring true. And certainly, committees do sometimes overlook fine teachers working part time on their own campuses. Some committee members may even harbor a bias against hiring adjuncts. But to suggest that committees in general are closed-minded when it comes to interviewing and hiring part-timers is simply mistaken.

At 4-year institutions, departments may well turn up their noses at hiring their own adjuncts. But the fact is, at community colleges, adjuncts have certain built-in advantages when they apply for full-time positions. They're known quantities. They may boast well-deserved reputations as outstanding teachers. They often have friends on the search committee who will advocate for them. As Betsy points out, they're familiar with the college's mission and understand what it means to teach at a 2-year college—something other applicants often don't. They may even have won teaching awards or earned accolades for valuable service to the college. On the other hand, adjuncts usually lack the full-time teaching experience that search committees seek— and that is stipulated in the official job description. And sometimes being a known quantity isn't entirely a good thing.

Outside applicants, meanwhile, especially if they're coming from other 2-year colleges, often do have the requisite experience. They probably also have a pretty good understanding of the community college mission and a feel for what the search committee is looking for. In addition, they may bring a fresh perspective that committee members find appealing. If they have taught full time for some years, they're probably highly capable teachers and can show that in the teaching-demonstration portion of the interview.

And yet they are outsiders. Their teaching philosophies and methodologies might differ from prevailing norms on the hiring campus. Questions about their motives for leaving other jobs, even if unasked, can linger in committee members' minds. And ultimately, hiring candidates from outside the institution might be seen as a bit of a gamble, since no one on the hiring committee really knows them. So the truth is that neither adjuncts nor outside applicants have a definitive edge in the hiring process. Both bring some positive attributes to the table, and both come with built-in drawbacks. Search committees have to weigh all of those factors when deciding whom to interview and, ultimately, hire.

Still, the anger persists on both sides—mostly, I think, because people don't understand the hiring process and haven't done the mental math. When a 2-year college advertises a tenure-track position, it's likely to receive more than 100 applications, from both internal and external candidates. Given those numbers, there's no way a search committee can make everyone happy—and that's not its job.

A few years ago, I chaired a search committee charged with evaluating 174 applicants for four positions. My college is a large one, with a correspondingly large number of adjuncts—and more than a third of them applied, constituting over half of the applicant pool. I think you can see where this is headed. As a committee, we decided to interview 12 candidates, which (as you know if you've ever sat through a day of interviews) is a lot. Still, with about 90 adjuncts applying, there was obviously no way we could interview all of them, or even most. Plus, we had quite a few promising external candidates and we wanted to interview some of them, too.

As I recall, we interviewed five or six of our own adjuncts and six or seven external applicants. We ended up hiring two of our adjuncts and two people from outside. That wasn't by design, and it certainly wasn't reflective of any quota; it's just the way it worked out—and it was fairly typical of how such searches work out.

That was little consolation to the 88 adjuncts who applied but didn't get full-time positions. Most of them took it pretty well. A few of them didn't. No doubt plenty of outside applicants weren't too happy about not being hired, either. They just didn't find my office nearly as accessible. Fortunately for them, there's always e-mail.

References

Jenkins, R. (2008, November 17). What community colleges want, part 2. *The Chronicle of Higher Education*. Available from http://www.chroniclecareers. com/article/what-community-colleges-want/45838/

Smith, B. (2008, December 5). The professor you need may be down the hall [Letter to the editor]. *The Chronicle of Higher Education*. Available from http:// www.chroniclecareers.com/article/the-professor-you-need-may-be/9586/

The original essay was published April 17, 2009, in *The Chronicle of Higher Education*.

Part 3

On Interviewing at a Community College

"ANY SPECIAL AWARDS OR HONORS OTHER THAN THE THREE GOLD STARS YOU GOT IN SECOND GRADE?"

When I talk about "getting a foot in the door," I really mean the door to the profession, not to any particular institution.

A FOOT IN THE DOOR AT COMMUNITY COLLEGES

"If you could offer me any advice on how to 'break in' to the community college market with a master's degree and two years of teaching experience, that would be great." "I've been teaching part time at a community college since 1999. What do I have to do to get a full-time job?" Those comments are typical of the responses I've received to my essays on teaching careers at 2-year colleges. Many people ask some version of the question posed by the first writer: How do I "break in?"

I can relate to their problem on a number of levels: as a career faculty member at community colleges who has taught both full time and part time, as a department head, and as a member (or chairman) of at least a dozen search committees. I'm also well aware that at this point in the academic year—after most of the interviews have been completed and most of the tenure-track jobs offered—there are many qualified people asking themselves this exact question, some in frustration or worse.

The people who put the question to me can be divided into roughly two groups: The first is made up of those with little or no experience teaching at community colleges, including recent graduates with master's and doctoral degrees and non-academic professionals looking to make a career change. The second group involves those who have been teaching part time at 2-year colleges for years and want (some desperately) to move into a full-time position. I'd like to address both groups.

If you're fresh out of graduate school and want to teach full time at a 2-year college, the main thing you need to understand is that the culture there is likely to be different from what you're used to, or what you may have daydreamed about. Very few faculty members at community colleges work in ivory towers; for the most part, we're laboring in the trenches. I tell you that because an ivory-tower view of academic life tends to manifest itself in a candidate's application materials and especially during the interview. Nothing dooms a candidacy more quickly, or more surely, than for the search committee to suspect that the applicant is mistaking a community college for a research institution—or, worse, that the applicant knows the difference but would greatly prefer the latter. Such a candidate must be either elitist and condescending or else hopelessly naïve, the committee concludes, and who wants to work with someone like that?

Whether you're coming from graduate school or from a nonacademic profession, the jargon of the community college setting might be new to you. Do you know what "developmental studies" entail? Are you familiar with "exit testing" and "cut scores"? Do you know the difference between an associate degree in science and one in applied science? You should, if you're planning to interview at 2-year colleges.

One of the best ways to prepare yourself for our job market is to teach part time at a 2-year college. That's true for any applicant—whether you're a new degree holder or a midlife career changer—and it shouldn't be too difficult to do so. No matter where you live, chances are there's a 2-year campus within easy driving distance. Since most of these colleges rely heavily on part-time instructors, you stand a good chance of getting hired as an adjunct, assuming you have at least a master's degree.

A part-time gig can be especially beneficial if you avail yourself of the opportunity to interact with some of your full-time colleagues at the college. They might seem a bit standoffish at first, but that's just because they don't know you. Once you get over that hump, you'll find that, over all, community college faculty members are a pretty friendly bunch. For the most part, they don't look down on part timers, since many full timers started out that way themselves. Engaging in conversations with your new colleagues—or merely listening in on their conversations about pedagogy and other daily concerns—will go a long way toward helping you master the jargon, so that you'll sound like a 2-year college veteran when you get a chance to interview for a full-time job.

In the interest of full disclosure, I should say one more thing about teaching part time: It will not necessarily help you get a full-time job at that same institution. At my college, for example, we have literally dozens of part-time English instructors, most of whom do a wonderful job. Each year, when we advertise two or three tenure-track openings, a large number of those adjuncts apply. Obviously, we can't even interview, much less hire, all of them, though it's not unusual for several to get interviews and one or two to get jobs. But the rest are understandably disappointed, sometimes even bitter, as if they assumed their part-time status guaranteed them something more. It doesn't.

So when I talk about "getting a foot in the door," I really mean the door to the profession, not to any particular institution. Your part-time teaching experience at a community college will almost certainly look good on your résumé, even if you are applying for full-time openings at 4-year colleges. In terms of community colleges, it will give you a better sense of what working at one is really like and make you a more viable—and desirable—candidate in the long run. So while a part-time stint at a 2-year college won't guarantee you a full-time job on that campus, it may well help you land one elsewhere.

Perhaps you're already teaching part time at a 2-year college and, like many in that situation, you'd love to move into a tenure-track job on the campus. Maybe you've been trying to do that for several years, without success. I do have some advice for you, although I fear you might not like it.

Frankly, you might want to consider moving. I say this knowing that many long-term part timers have deep ties to the communities where they live, including children in school and spouses who work nearby. But the reality of the job market is that, if you're focusing your search on a single institution, or even two or three in the same geographic area, you're statistically much less likely to land a tenure-track job than someone who is willing to move across the country. Ultimately, the question is one of priorities: Live where you prefer and continue teaching part time, perhaps indefinitely, or give up the life you've established for a tenure-track job someplace else.

If you choose the former—if you can't or simply don't want to move—there are things you can do to increase your chances of getting a full-time position at the college (or one of the colleges) where you now teach part time. First, understand that landing a full-time job will be a long-term process. Don't give up when you don't get hired (or even get an interview) the first year or two that you apply. It might take four or five years, sometimes even longer, for you to show up on the search committee's radar. But if that's where you want to work, and you keep applying year after year, your persistence alone will eventually set you apart from most of your part-time colleagues, many of whom will give up after the first year or two.

Meanwhile, get to know as many of your full-time colleagues as you can. When a search committee is formed, the full timers are the ones who will be on it, and the more people you know on the committee (who have a high opinion of you), the better. To the extent that you're able, given your teaching schedule and other commitments, make yourself a fixture in the department. Attend departmental meetings, volunteer to help out with the drearier departmental tasks, socialize with your colleagues.

Complete the training required of faculty advisers and offer to help with that often-unpopular duty, if your college will allow it. Not only will you be gaining valuable experience and establishing contacts that could be helpful later on, you'll also be able to include that experience in your cover letter and résumé when you next apply. Finally, become as engaged as you can in service and professional development, the two primary responsibilities of 2-year college faculty members outside of teaching. Many campuses welcome the involvement of part timers on certain committees, and some colleges even have committees composed primarily of part-time faculty members. Seek out such assignments. Find out what kinds of technological or pedagogical training opportunities at your campus are open to part timers and sign up. There may even be local professional conferences you can attend at minimal cost.

Again, all these activities will help you strengthen your résumé, increase your understanding of the 2-year college environment, and establish valuable relationships. Ultimately, it may be those relationships, and your understanding of how the college works, even more than your résumé, that will get your foot in the tenure-track door.

The original essay was published April 12, 2004, in *The Chronicle of Higher Education*.

Your knowledge of the institution, the department, and the community should give you a good idea of exactly what they're looking for and enable you to present yourself as a strong candidate. Remember to emphasize your teaching experience and try to relate it to the job description.

INTERVIEWING AT A TWO-YEAR COLLEGE

f you took the advice in my essays about applying for teaching jobs at 2-year colleges, and if you're a strong candidate for those jobs (not to mention a bit lucky), you should soon start hearing from search committees. Understand that when I say "soon," I mean that in relative terms. This is higher education we're talking about, after all. Maybe you'll hear something in a few months.

Volumes have been written about how to conduct yourself in a job interview, including much good advice on how to dress, how to modulate your voice, and so on. (See Dana M. Zimbleman's excellent piece, "Interviewing for a Job at a Community College," in *The Chronicle of Higher Education*, July 16, 2002). She covers some ground—about teaching demonstrations, for example—that I'm going to retread only briefly here.) What I want to talk about is that period between the telephone call inviting you for an interview and the interview itself. That, in my estimation, is the most crucial part of the entire job-search process. What you do with that time will determine how well you come across in the interview and, ultimately, whether you have a legitimate shot at the job.

The caller—usually the head of the search committee but perhaps a secretary—will first ask if you're still interested in the position, and then offer you an interview slot. Take the earliest time available, when committee members will still be fresh, both mentally and physically. (Understand that they may be interviewing as many as 8 or 10 candidates for a single job.) If your performance is particularly strong, you could set a standard against which subsequent candidates will compare unfavorably.

You may also chat about other things, such as travel expenses (some 2-year colleges pay them, some don't), directions to the campus, and the weather (hey, search committee chairs are people, too). Just be sure you write down the caller's name, title, and telephone number before you hang up. That information could come in handy at any number of points down the road, such as when your car breaks down on the way to the interview.

A week or two after the call, you should receive a letter from the committee confirming your appointment and containing other useful information. If the letter is correct in its particulars, accurately reflecting what you discussed on the phone, there's no need to acknowledge it. Only if details are wrong or missing—such as the college's commitment to cover your travel expenses—should you call or e-mail. (Personally, I prefer e-mail; it's less intrusive, and I can answer it at my leisure.)

The letter should also give you a better idea of what will be expected of you during the interview. For example, many 2-year colleges include a teaching demonstration as part of the interview. The letter should tell you if that's the case and give you some ideas about the topic, the time limit, and the availability of resources (in case you plan on using technology during your demonstration).

Most colleges include, along with the confirmation letter, a hefty information packet—catalog, brochures, area maps, and so forth. Plan on spending a lot of time with these documents, familiarizing yourself with the college and the local community as much as possible. The first thing you should do is pinpoint the exact location of the campus, especially if you're driving. Then study such items as course offerings, student and faculty demographics, and the college's history and mission statement. Go online and look at the Web pages of departments and individual faculty members. All of this will give you an appreciation for the place and its culture that will be readily apparent to the committee members during the interview.

You should also begin preparing for some of the questions you might be asked during the interview. Every search is different, and I can't claim to predict which questions you'll be asked. But over the years, as a candidate and as a committee member, I've noticed certain ones that usually come up. For example, the committee will probably ask you about your academic preparation and experience. Obviously, this is all laid out in detail in your résumé and cover letter. During the interview, what they're really asking is what would make you a good fit for their institution. Here's where good preparation will serve you well: Your knowledge of the institution, the department, and the community should give you a good idea of exactly what they're looking for and enable you to present yourself as a strong candidate. Remember to emphasize your teaching experience and try to relate it to the job description.

You can also expect questions about your experience with diverse student populations (2-year colleges tend to be more diverse than any other type of postsecondary institution), your familiarity with and use of technology in and out of the classroom, and your approach to teaching underprepared students. You might even get one of those annoying "strengths/weaknesses" questions. If so, use a discussion of strengths to emphasize your commitment to teaching and learning. Under weaknesses, merely talk about the negative side of some of your strengths—for example, maybe you spend too much time grading, or you are sometimes too trusting of students.

Another important way to occupy your time between the telephone call and the interview is to prepare your teaching demonstration. Most committees will ask you to talk for 10 to 15 minutes about a specified topic or about one of your choosing. Understand that what they're almost certainly looking for is a 15-minute segment of a lesson, not a 15-minute synopsis of an entire class.

One of the most common mistakes candidates make during this portion of the interview is to tell the committee what they would do if they had more time, instead of spending the time they have actually doing it. Remember, this is a demonstration, not a presentation. Imagine the committee members as your "students," and use your 15 minutes to leave no doubt in their minds as to your effectiveness in the classroom.

Finally, you should prepare a list of short, incisive questions for the committee. I regularly judge candidates as much by what they ask us as by how they respond to our interrogation. You have to be careful with your questions. Asking about time off for research (there won't be any) will make you appear better suited for a research institution. Asking about the workload might suggest that you're lazy, especially if your face registers shock at the answer. (That information should be available on the college's Web site, anyway, if you look hard enough.) And the interview isn't the place, in my opinion, to ask specific questions about salary and benefits. That comes when you're offered the job—though again, you can probably get a general idea beforehand by searching the Web.

You can, however, ask about the college's support for faculty travel to conferences, about training opportunities on the campus, and about tuition reimbursement for faculty members taking additional graduate courses. Ask which types of courses you would be expected to teach and how those courses are assigned. Ask about committee work and other opportunities for service. Such questions signal to me that candidates have a pretty good idea of what they are getting themselves into.

You can also ask questions that highlight your knowledge of the institution, acquired through weeks of Web-browsing and poring over often-tedious college publications. For example: "I see from your last annual report that enrollment has grown more than 25% in the past two years. To what do you attribute that growth?" Or how about a question like this, illustrating not only your knowledge but your enthusiasm: "I noticed when reading up on the college's shared governance structure that each discipline has its own curriculum committee. Are junior faculty members allowed to serve?"

I don't mean to sound disingenuous or cynical. I hope you are genuinely interested in serving on curriculum committees, just as I hope your weaknesses are merely counterpoints to your strengths. Experienced faculty members on the search committee will no doubt be quick to sniff out any hint of obsequiousness or insincerity. But if you are an excellent teacher with enthusiasm for your subject and a yen to teach at a 2-year college, we want to know. I've seen too many promising candidates—people who I know are good teachers—fail to get full-time jobs because they didn't do well in an interview. One way to prevent that, I believe, is by being well prepared. There's no reason not to be: You've got all the information you'll ever need right at your fingertips and two or three weeks (at least) before your date with the committee. Use the time wisely.

References

Zimbleman, Dana M. (2002, July 16). Interviewing for a job at a community college. *The Chronicle of Higher Education.* Available from http://www.chroniclecareers.com/article/Interviewing-for-a-Job-at-a/46153/

The original essay was published January 15, 2004, in *The Chronicle of Higher Education.*

> One of the main reasons that otherwise-viable candidates do poorly in an interview is that they don't understand community colleges. They're unfamiliar with our values and don't speak our jargon.

THE COMMUNITY COLLEGE INTERVIEW

As you prepare for an interview at a 2-year college, keep in mind that your chances of getting the job depend more on your ability to speak the language of community colleges than on any other single factor. In my experience—23 years as a faculty member, department head, and dean at 2-year colleges—one of the main reasons that otherwise-viable candidates do poorly in an interview is that they don't understand community colleges. They're unfamiliar with our values and don't speak our jargon.

Do you know what "the community college mission" is? Do you understand what faculty members at 2-year colleges mean when we talk about "teaching and learning" or "the learning campus"? Are you familiar with various learning styles, and can you identify them and explain to the committee how you would accommodate each in your teaching? And what will you answer when a committee member asks about your "use of technology in the classroom"? Those are among the phrases that, I've found, either leave candidates looking confused or elicit responses that have nothing to do with the question.

Take the matter of the community college mission. You may be required to discuss that topic in writing, as part of the application process, or be asked to talk about it during the interview. Not to be glib, but you can't go wrong with some variation on the following response: "Community colleges meet students where they are and take them where they need to go." Because that's the simple truth. Bear in mind that nearly all 2-year colleges have "open-door" policies, meaning they accept anyone with a high school or General Educational Development diploma, regardless of grade-point average or SAT scores. Many enroll non–high school graduates in adult education programs.

At the same time, community colleges in many states are expected to show graduation and persistence rates similar to those of their more selective, better-financed, 4-year sister institutions. So when you apply to a 2-year college, you had better be able to teach. You'd better be able to meet students where they are and take them where they need to go, both for the students' sake and for the sake of the college. By and large, community colleges do a remarkable and largely unheralded job of fulfilling that mission.

It's important for you as a candidate to understand, then, that even though some of your students may be above average in terms of intellectual ability and academic preparation, you will also have some who are going to require all of your teaching skills to reach. It's even more important for the search committee to recognize that you understand and embrace that fact—that you're not just another research-oriented, frustrated job seeker "settling" for a position at a 2-year college.

The mission of the community college is not just teaching, it's also learning. That may sound suspiciously like academic doublespeak. It's not. When we talk about teaching and learning or about the learning campus, we're really emphasizing, once again, the primary mission of the college: not merely to teach, but to ensure that students learn. Community colleges have a vested interest in that process that goes beyond the professionalism and compassion of individual instructors. Whereas certain professors or programs at more selective institutions may take pride in "weeding out" those students who "can't cut it," community colleges and their faculties are committed both by charter and by disposition to helping every student "cut it."

The focus is not on the professor, but on the student, the learner. Faculty members at 2-year colleges are both trained and predisposed to consider the student first when developing course materials, activities, even the overall approach to the course. We've learned that traditional methods of delivery, like lecture and class discussion, may work fine for some students in some situations but might not be sufficient to help every student master the material. That kind of extra attention to the learning process is both expected by the institution and, in most cases, personally important to the faculty member.

Which brings me to "learning styles." Research has shown that not all people learn in the same way. Some learn best by listening, others by reading. Some are highly visual, others more hands on. Good teachers understand that their students come to them with different learning styles and incorporate into their teaching approach activities that appeal to each style—as opposed to merely lecturing, which reaches only auditory learners.

Search committees at 2-year colleges will expect you to have at least some familiarity with learning-styles research and to have given some thought as to how you might deal with different styles in your classroom. I would recommend that you *not* rely on my one-paragraph synopsis. Do your own research.

Finally we come to the issue of technology, as in "Tell us how you use technology in your classroom." I've heard too many candidates respond to that question by mumbling something about e-mail or talking about how their students have to write their term papers on a computer. Those answers are not going to impress us. That's because, despite our annual budget contortions, many community colleges are remarkably advanced technologically. That may be, in part, because we teach so many courses in information technology and related fields. Or perhaps, given our student-focused approach, we simply spend what money we have on tools for improving teaching.

Whatever the reason, a large percentage of community college classrooms contain at least one computer and a data projector, while many are fully outfitted for 25 or 30 students. A surprising number even have interactive whiteboard technology. I say surprising because surprise is often the reaction when friends and colleagues from research universities visit our campus. They're shocked to find that our classrooms are, by and large, better equipped than theirs. It's no wonder, then, that many first-time candidates for 2-year college teaching jobs, who, as graduate assistants, were probably relegated to the worst rooms on the campus, have no idea what we mean by "using technology in the classroom."

Understand that, for us, technology is a tool—possibly the primary tool—for transforming the classroom from the traditional "sage on the stage" to a true learning-centered environment. Through selective use of Internet resources, streaming video, and presentation software, to name a few applications, instructors create engaging, interactive lessons that appeal to a variety of learners. Of course, not all instructors use those tools, and some use them far more than others. But community colleges are definitely looking for new faculty members who both can, and will, use them.

That said, it isn't absolutely necessary for you to know how to manipulate a SmartBoard or have experience with streaming video going into the interview. If your community college campus is as wired as most, you will have ample training opportunities once you're hired. The important thing is that you understand what those tools are for and demonstrate a willingness to use them.

Armed with a new vocabulary—and bolstered by your own research—you should come across in your interview as someone who knows what 2-year colleges are all about and who shares our vision. My hope, of course, is that you will actually become that person, not merely present yourself as such. More than anything else—even more than new computers—we need excellent teachers who are committed to the community college mission. If that describes you, I wish you the best of luck.

The original essay was published February 17, 2006, in *The Chronicle of Higher Education*.

> I've watched a parade of clueless job candidates—
> all of them neatly groomed, appropriately dressed,
> well mannered, and painfully earnest—become
> sad victims of unwitting self-sabotage.

THE COMMUNITY COLLEGE INTERVIEW: WHAT NOT TO DO

Speaking as someone who has interviewed scores of candidates for teaching positions at 2-year colleges, and who will no doubt be interviewing dozens more over the next few years, I would just like to say: Please, shoot me now. Of course, I'm kidding—kind of. But community college professors who, like me, have sat on search committee after search committee, year after year, know exactly what I'm talking about.

We all understand how important it is to serve. We recognize the opportunity it presents to have a say in the direction of the department. None of that changes the fact that it's basically a tiresome, tedious, thankless job. However, this column is not for the jaded tenured professors out there nodding their heads in agreement. Nor is it for those who, perversely, enjoy serving on search committees and are even now composing indignant e-mail rejoinders in their heads.

No, this column is for all you bright-eyed, idealistic job seekers, most likely young and fresh out of graduate school, who will be sitting down across from us in a few weeks, totally oblivious to our cynicism. You probably don't realize that, after the third or fourth interview, you all start to sound alike. You probably don't know that, even as we stare at you over the conference table, we're actually wishing we were somewhere else, such as a dentist's office or a branch location of the Internal Revenue Service.

What I'm offering you, the candidate, in this column is an opportunity to stand out from the crowd, not based on anything you do but on what you *shouldn't* do. Heck, you already know what to do—how to dress, how to speak to the various people you meet, how to answer the important questions (what are your key weaknesses, anyway?), even how to shake hands. Scores of articles have been written on the subject, including at least one I wrote myself.

Even more important than what you say and how you act, however, may be what you don't say and the behaviors you manage to avoid. I've become increasingly convinced of that as I've watched a parade of clueless job candidates—all of them neatly groomed, appropriately dressed, well mannered, and painfully earnest—become sad victims of unwitting self-sabotage. Here, then, is my list of don'ts for your interview at a community college:

Don't Talk Too Much

One of the worst things you can do as a candidate is spend 20 minutes answering the first question—which, most likely, was not designed to inspire a 20-minute response. In fact, it's probably one of at least 10 questions the search committee would like to ask during your 60-minute interview. Taking too much time on the first one throws the entire interview off track, thereby irritating committee members—most of whom will stop listening to your rambling answer after the first five minutes, anyway.

We understand that candidates who give over-long answers usually do so because they're nervous and/or deathly afraid of leaving out something important. (I say usually; some are just long-winded.) But just because we understand doesn't mean our patience and credulity won't be sorely taxed. The best way to avoid talking too much is to be as prepared as possible. If you have a pretty good idea what you might be asked going into an interview—and you'll find lists of likely questions in a variety of sources—you can craft answers in advance that will be responsive, yet to the point.

You'll have, in other words, no need to ramble on. True, your answers may appear a bit rehearsed, but trust me on this: Rehearsed is better than long-winded. And if you're surprised by a question, or don't know a good answer, the worst thing you can do is attempt to expound at length anyway. You won't be fooling anyone in the room. As professors, we know bloviating when we hear it. So just give the shortest answer possible—even if it's "That's not something I'm real familiar with at this point"—and move on. The low marks for that answer will be offset by brownie points for not wasting people's time, trying their patience, and insulting their intelligence.

Don't Forget Where You Are

I know that may sound like strange advice, since you'll probably spend weeks planning your trip, plotting the college's exact location on the map, and reading about it on the Web. No doubt you'll also spend a great deal of time studying up on 2-year colleges, so that you understand how they differ from 4-year, research institutions. Even so, I've found that a distressingly large number of candidates fail to take the most basic steps to familiarize themselves with our college. Or maybe during the interview they suffer a sudden attack of instant-onset amnesia. The most common symptom, among newly minted PhDs, is a tendency to launch into a protracted exegesis of their dissertation and discussion of research interests.

Look, the fact that you wrote a dissertation is probably, in the eyes of most committee members, a plus. But beyond that—and I don't mean this unkindly—we don't care. Two-year colleges are teaching institutions, plain and simple. And as search committee members, we're looking for the best teachers (and best colleagues) we can find who meet the minimum job requirements—usually, a master's degree with 18 graduate semester hours in the teaching discipline. It's not that we're averse to hiring PhDs, or to having colleagues who like to do research. We just regard any time you spend talking about those things during your interview as time you could have spent talking about your teaching, or time we could have spent taking a much-needed bathroom break.

Don't Patronize Your Interviewers

Some of you are probably wondering to yourselves, "Who would do that?" The answer is, a lot of candidates. Let's be honest. Statistically speaking, most of you applied for faculty positions at community colleges because the academic market is tough and you need a job. Teaching at a 2-year college probably isn't your first choice. If you actually get the job, you may well find that you enjoy the environment. But you aren't thinking about that during the interview. You're just thinking about making a decent living and having affordable health insurance.

More to the point, your decision to apply to 2-year colleges may not have sat too well with your dissertation adviser, or been popular with the other graduate students in your program. Maybe they told you that you were "selling yourself short" or "casting your pearls before swine." Unfortunately, their negative attitude toward community colleges may well have rubbed off on you. If so, that's likely to become apparent at some point during the interview, unless you will yourself to avoid it.

So be careful what you say and how you say it. Don't drop names of prominent people in your field whom you've met at conferences. Don't ramble on about all the millions of dollars your university invests in your discipline. Resist the urge to make lofty pronouncements about your specialty, assuming that because committee members are "just" community college professors, they don't know as much about the field as you do. (Hint: Many of them do.) You should even watch your body language. Don't react with surprise and dismay—or outright disgust—when confronted with the realities of academic life at a 2-year college: a teaching load of five courses a semester, no research assistants, minuscule travel budgets. If you've done your homework, you will know those things already.

The bottom line is, if you look down on community colleges and don't really want to teach here, why interview? And if the answer is "because I need the job," then, at the very least, don't let your condescension become visible. And if you do, don't be surprised when the search committee regards you as someone without whom their institution would get along just fine. If, on the other hand, you manage to avoid talking yourself out of consideration, if you remember where you are, and if you at least feign respect for committee members, you might just survive this whole community college interview thing. More important, those of us sitting across the table from you might just survive it, too.

The original essay was published February 11, 2008, in *The Chronicle of Higher Education.*

> Use your interview to show us you're an outstanding teacher, and you stand a good chance of being hired.

HOW TO STAND OUT IN YOUR INTERVIEW

If you were successful in following the advice in my earlier essay, "How to Make Your Application Stand Out," you're probably preparing for an interview at a community college this spring, or at least you will be at some point. Now comes the real challenge: continuing to stand out among a group of candidates whose applications were all impressive to the committee. I've participated in scores of job interviews, as a candidate and as a member of at least 15 search committees that I can recall (some of my committee experiences I've repressed, no doubt). Since I've been an administrator, I've also worked behind the scenes, scheduling interviews, developing questions, and reviewing committee recommendations. So I have a pretty fair idea of what it takes to stand out in an interview at 2-year colleges.

Timing

The date and time of your interview are more important than you might think. The timing is, in any case, the first decision you'll have to make about the interview, assuming you have a choice. You won't always. Some committees will give you a "take it or leave it" date and time. Others might simply get to you last as they're phoning candidates, so that you have to take whatever time slot is left. You shouldn't read too much into that; it probably has to do with the order the folders were in when they were handed to whoever made the calls. Interview scheduling is, at best, an inexact science.

But if you do get to choose a time for your interview, my advice is to select the earliest slot available, if the interviews are being conducted in a single day or on consecutive days. (You can ask the person who calls how the schedule is set up.) If the interview dates are separated by a week or more, choose the earliest slot on the last day. To follow my reasoning, you have to understand that most 2-year colleges conduct what I call "cattle call" interviews, scheduling five, six, or more 1-hour slots in a single day. Often we try to interview all the candidates on that one day, or over a 2-day period.

That means that, by the end of the day—not to mention the second day—we're pretty bushed, and all the interviews start to run together. You stand a better chance of making a good impression if you get to us while we're still relatively fresh. On the other hand (speaking as a serial committee member), if I've had a week to recover, I find that I'm more likely to remember the people we interviewed on the last day—as long as they didn't come too late in the day.

The last thing I'll say about timing is this: Show up at least 30 minutes early. An hour is better. If you find that you're too early, you can spend the time profitably wandering around the campus, which may help you get a better feel for the job. (Just don't get lost.) No one will think badly of you for being early, unless maybe you show up the night before and camp on the lawn.

Appearance

It's important, when interviewing for a faculty position, is to appear professional without looking too corporate—although women can pull off businesslike better than men. A woman in a dark suit looks professional. A man in a dark suit looks like an accountant, or maybe an undertaker.

For men, then, I recommend a sport coat, dress slacks, and tie: perhaps something classic, like a navy blazer over a blue oxford shirt and gray flannels, or something professorial, like a brown tweed jacket with tan slacks. Shirts should be white or light blue only, while ties should be understated in pattern and color. Also, wear dress shoes that go with your slacks—brown with tan, black with gray or navy—and that have been polished in recent memory.

For women, a dark suit is always appropriate, although it should probably be offset by a colorful blouse. (Women can get away with a lot more color than men.) Or you can go with the feminine equivalent of the classic or professorial looks described above. Slacks are generally better than skirts, and dresses are usually a bad idea. Shoes should be conservative in style and height.

Pay attention to your personal grooming, too. These days, a man's hair can be any length, but it should be well kept. The same goes for facial hair. Women should avoid extremes in hairstyles, makeup, and jewelry. Dress appropriately, and when you walk into the interview room, you will send the message that you are someone to be taken seriously.

Performance

The single most important factor, of course, is how well you actually perform during the interview. You need to display the right balance of confidence and humility—confidence in your abilities and preparation, but deference to the interviewers who certainly know more about the institution than you do and probably have more years in the profession. One way to gain confidence is to learn everything you can, before the interview, about the institution and about community colleges. That way, you can give an intelligent answer to a question like "How would you teach such-and-such in a developmental-studies course?" If your answer is "A developmental-studies course?" followed by a blank look, the interview isn't going well.

As you answer questions, focus on your teaching experience, as opposed to your research, as much as possible. (An obvious point, you say? Not judging by the number of candidates who come to a community college interview and talk far too much about their scholarship.) If you wrote a dissertation and earned a PhD, the committee members are probably impressed; it may even be one of the reasons they invited you for an interview. But they don't necessarily want to hear about a research agenda that likely has little to do with what you'll actually be doing on the job every day. Instead, they'd like to hear as much as possible about your teaching.

A key element of the job interview at most 2-year colleges is the teaching demonstration. I cover that in an essay titled "Demonstration or Demolition?" and for the sake of space I won't recap it all here. Suffice it to say, the committee is hoping for a demonstration of your teaching ability, not a conference presentation on some discipline-related topic. They want to see you teach, not hear about how you would teach. So choose a 15- to 20-minute segment of a lecture you're comfortable giving and approach it just like you would if you were in a classroom.

Finally, if you have the chance at the conclusion of the interview, ask sharp questions. It is OK to ask about things like the salary range and benefits, if those haven't already been discussed (and they should have been). You can also ask about the possibility of summer teaching assignments, requirements for tenure and promotion, and even workload. Just try not to blanch when someone says you'll be teaching five courses each semester.

Remember, even though we're in a recession and the job market basically stinks, community college enrollments are still growing, and we continue to need new faculty members. Use your interview to show us you're an outstanding teacher, and you stand a good chance of being hired.

The original essay was published February 15, 2010, in *The Chronicle of Higher Education.*

Yahoo! Here's one who doesn't meet the experience requirement. One less folder to read through.

CATTLE CALL

You know it's coming. Any day now you'll get that telephone call or e-mail message asking you to serve on yet another search committee. As a tenure-track faculty member at a 2-year college, you'll most likely say yes. Here you go again.

I'm not going to recite platitudes about the joys of service or bore you with legalities. I'm sure your college, like mine, employs professionals to do that. Instead, I'd like to share some complaints from real job seekers who have e-mailed me over the past year to voice their frustrations with the hiring process at community colleges.

Too often those of us who serve on search committees come to see applicants as mere file folders—or worse, as nuisances—rather than as actual people. I've been guilty of that myself. So let's remind ourselves that we're dealing with human beings, over whose lives we have temporarily, and more or less randomly, been assigned some measure of control. We must accept that responsibility with soberness and humility, not arrogance or barely disguised annoyance.

We should also remember that the process of searching for new faculty members is supposed to be mutually beneficial to both the hirer and the person hired. The candidates bring important qualities to the table, qualities we are, or should be, looking for. They come to us hoping to establish careers at our institutions and build lives in our communities. Committee members, for their part, seek to enhance the academic, intellectual, and social environments of their campuses by hiring the best teachers and colleagues.

In the end, even those candidates who don't get hired should come out of the process feeling that, at a minimum, they were treated with respect and that, ideally, they learned and grew from the experience. Sadly, that's not usually the case. Sometimes our searches are more like "cattle calls," as one frustrated job seeker put it. "I appreciate your attempts to help prepare people interviewing for positions at community colleges," she says, "but perhaps what's really needed is better-informed search committee members and chairs."

The complaints I received focused primarily on two issues. The first is salary, and specifically, the fact that many search committees won't talk about it. "I wonder," wrote one reader, "if a committee remaining so 'tight-lipped' about something as basic as salary is not hiding other things." The second concern of job candidates involves their perception that many community colleges are unwilling to give "inexperienced," first-time teachers a chance. "What I found most frustrating about seeking community college employment," wrote another reader, "is that, unlike almost all other careers, community college teaching does not seem to have an entry level. Community colleges simply do not hire beginning teachers."

At first glance, it seems there's nothing an individual faculty member serving on a search committee can do about either of those complaints. Or is there? Let's take the salary issue first. Several readers wrote to say that they felt it was unreasonable for candidates not to be told the starting salary for a position during the interview (if not before), or at least given a range. So why are search committees often reluctant to talk about money?

The answer is probably because they've been told not to, but that seems like a lame excuse. Can a community college really expect people to make potentially life-changing decisions, to contemplate moving their families across the country, based solely on the notion that teaching is its own reward? Maybe individual committee members can't do anything about the fact that the college didn't mention salary in the position announcement, as it should have. But you can resolve among yourselves to be forthright with candidates on the subject. So disclose the salary. You can always cover yourself with the caveat, "Of course, human resources will determine your exact salary," but at least give a range.

The second brings up higher education's version of an age-old conundrum: How do you get a job without experience, and how do you get experience without a job? As another astute and frustrated reader observed, "From the point of view of the search committee, I know the reason [why community colleges don't hire beginning teachers]: The pool always contains plenty of experienced applicants, and, all else being equal, experience wins. From an applicant's point of view, though, this is maddening."

My college has been struggling recently with this very problem. For the past few years, we've made "three years full-time teaching experience" a required qualification in our job advertisements for new tenure-track faculty members. That has led some of us who frequently serve on search committees to wonder if we're missing out on some of the best talent right out of graduate school—promising young scholars whom many 4-year colleges would not hesitate to hire.

I know of one case involving a candidate we really wanted, a young woman with otherwise impeccable credentials who had only two years of teaching experience. Fortunately, we were able to hire her in a temporary position, which both sides hope is eventually converted to tenure track. But we nearly lost her.

To avoid losing promising young faculty members, the long-term solution, from an institutional point of view, is to rewrite your job descriptions and either eliminate the experience requirement altogether or at least deemphasize it. Maybe you could move teaching experience from the "required" list to the "desired" list, or perhaps you could simply lighten up—require one year of previous experience in the classroom instead of two or three, with two years of part-time teaching counting as one year of full-time.

Of course, once again, individual search committee members can't do much about the way the job ad was written. But perhaps the members of the committee can agree to consider more carefully those applicants who are borderline in the experience department—or maybe even below borderline—rather than simply rejecting them out of hand as an easy way to narrow the field. ("Yahoo! Here's one who doesn't meet the experience requirement. One less folder to read through." Not that that would ever happen.) And if the committee members find that the best candidate is someone who doesn't have the required experience, perhaps they can go together to the department head or the dean and plead that applicant's case. Few administrators, I think, could withstand the joint plea of several determined tenured faculty members.

Once the search is over, committee members can also take up the experience requirement with their administrations. Ultimately faculty members hire new faculty members—at least, we do all the grunt work. And we're the ones who have to work with new colleagues and advise them. It's in the long-term best interests of our colleges to reintroduce the entry-level position into the community college job market. Right now there may be far more applicants than jobs, so we can pick and choose.

But that might not always be the case. As our older colleagues retire, and as the number of students attending 2-year colleges continues to grow, we will need constant infusions of new blood, in the form of new young faculty members. It doesn't make sense for us to ignore those who might become some of our best teachers (and friends), just because they are neophyte teachers fresh out of graduate school.

In the end, serving on a search committee may turn out to be the most important thing you did this year, professionally speaking. I hope you will approach the task with sensitivity and an open mind. I hope your applicant pool is deep, filled both with experienced professors seeking a change of venue and with eager young hopefuls plunging enthusiastically into the profession. Above all, I hope your top applicants refuse to schedule an interview unless you tell them the salary up front.

The original essay was published February 14, 2005, in *The Chronicle of Higher Education.*

Whatever your college's stance on shared governance, you can have a tremendous impact on the long-term effectiveness of your college—not to mention your own day-to-day job satisfaction—by making sure you choose the best teachers and the best colleagues you can.

FOR COMMUNITY COLLEGE INTERVIEWERS: WHAT NOT TO DO

The problem with the faculty hiring process at 2-year colleges isn't that candidates are unprepared or don't know how to behave during a job interview. The problem is that members of search committees tend to be arrogant, cynical, bored, and distracted. At least, that's the word from a number of readers who have responded to my essays advising candidates on what to do—or what not to do—in a job interview. The aforementioned readers, in turn, had a few suggestions for me, many of which are printable.

It was clear that most of my e-mail correspondents had been through numerous job searches and become frustrated by the process. A recurring theme in their remarks was, "That's easy for you to say. You have a job. Why don't you try being on the market for a while?" For the record, I have been on the job market, more than once. I've been interviewed at least a dozen times and landed tenure-track positions at four colleges. I'm well aware that that makes me one of the lucky ones, but I've also had to jump through the same hoops as everyone else and endure the same kind of stress and anxiety.

Where I may differ from many readers is that I've also spent a considerable amount of time on the other side of the table. In my 23 years as a faculty member and administrator at community colleges, I've participated in at least 10 searches for faculty members plus countless others for administrative and staff positions. That gives me, I believe, a rather unique perspective, one I've tried to share through my essays in "The Two-Year Track" advice column for *The Chronicle of Higher Education*. Those essays have generated a lot of good advice from readers that is worth passing on to others who, like me, frequently serve on search committees.

Many readers, for example, have pointed out that not all candidates are young people applying for their first community college job. That's hardly a revelation to experienced search committee members, but to the extent that we tend to lump all job seekers together, we probably need the occasional reminder. The fact is, in almost any batch of applications, at least half of the candidates are either long-term adjuncts of the college to which they have applied or experienced faculty members from other 2-year institutions. Far from being fresh-faced novices approaching the committee hat-in-hand, many applicants are established colleagues in their own right, likely to resent (and rightly so) any sign of condescension on the part of committee members.

Another point many readers made strongly (to say the least) is that committee members should treat job applicants like human beings—not as numbers or (as a long-time adjunct once said to me) like cattle being herded past stock-buyers at auction. While such advice should be unnecessary, as a practical matter, the "cattle call" mentality can be difficult to resist when you're interviewing six people in a single day, one right after the other. Even so, we must strive to be "humane," as one reader wrote. Candidates are people, with families, aspirations, and feelings. Sure, we have to be as objective as possible in our appraisals, but that doesn't mean we have to be cold. There's nothing to stop us from connecting and relating to job candidates on a personal level (without asking inappropriate questions, of course), regardless of whether we eventually hire them.

Several readers also said faculty members should keep in mind the reason they are serving on the search committee and the opportunity it presents. It may be, as I previously wrote, that working on a search committee is basically "a tiresome, tedious, thankless job." But that's no excuse for allowing our attention to waver or letting boredom get the better of us at any stage of the process. As academics, we've dealt with tedium all of our lives, in situations ranging from essay grading to faculty meetings to graduate seminars. We've trained ourselves, in the face of that boredom, to focus on the task at hand. Giving anything less than our full attention to a faculty search—by force of will, if necessary—is unprofessional and a disservice to the job applicants. Whatever your college's stance on shared governance, you can have a tremendous impact on the long-term effectiveness of your college—not to mention your own day-to-day job satisfaction—by making sure you choose the best teachers and the best colleagues you can.

And finally, as one of my correspondents reminded me, all of us who serve on search committees have to be careful not to let our biases affect our decisions. I'm not referring to extreme forms of bias, like racism or sexism. No doubt those still play a role in some searches, but they probably deserve a more thorough treatment than I can give them here. What I mean are the more subtle biases that we might not even recognize as such, involving concepts such as a candidate's teaching approach, professional or personal philosophy, and disciplinary theory. While it's perfectly appropriate to consider such intangibles when judging an applicant's candidacy, it's a mistake to let those considerations—which may actually be little more than visceral reactions—form the sole basis for our hiring decisions. In other words, we owe it to our colleges and to the candidates themselves to remain open-minded when confronted by people whose teaching strategies, disciplinary approaches, backgrounds, and ideas differ from our own.

Other biases may have to do with characteristics such as age—real or perceived—and appearance. Deciding not to hire candidates because we think they are too "immature," based on our assumptions about their age, is just as much a form of discrimination as hiring more-attractive candidates without regard for qualifications. Search committee members can even demonstrate bias against applicants who have been long-term adjuncts, wondering (aloud, at times) why they've never landed a full-time job. Or they can be biased in favor of certain candidates—adjuncts with whom they have become friendly over the years, or colleagues they have met at conferences.

Perhaps I can sum up the advice my readers gave me simply by paraphrasing the golden rule: As search committee members, we should treat candidates the way we would want to be treated if we were sitting on their side of the table. All the while, thanking our lucky stars that we're not.

The original essay was published March 12, 2008, in *The Chronicle of Higher Education*.

> Treating committee members as if they were students means forgetting, for a few minutes, that they hold your professional future in their hands and relating to them as you would to students in a classroom.

DEMONSTRATION OR DEMOLITION?

I f you're fortunate enough to have scored a job interview at a 2-year college, congratulations. Now it's time to start preparing for what is arguably the most important, probably the most arduous, and certainly the most daunting (judging from the e-mail messages I receive) part of the interview: the teaching demonstration. Over the course of my 23 years' teaching at community colleges, I've observed dozens of teaching demos. Only a few were actually good. Most were just OK, and many were downright awful. I've seen a number of otherwise-solid candidates derailed by their demonstrations, and many other people whom we hired despite a lackluster performance, hoping against hope that it was an aberration.

Those candidates were not bad teachers. OK, some of them were, but in most cases, the problem was not that they didn't know how to teach but rather that they didn't know how to conduct a teaching demonstration during a job interview. The two things, while obviously related, aren't exactly the same. Here, then, are some tips to remember as you prepare your teaching demo.

It's a Demonstration, Not a Presentation

One of the biggest mistakes job candidates make is treating the teaching demo like a conference talk, sometimes even complete with PowerPoint slides and handouts of those same slides. It's not that using technology is a bad idea (more on that later); it's just that candidates who are using it in that particular way are demonstrating the wrong thing. They're showing the committee how well they can present information to peers in a conference setting, not how well they can teach students in a college classroom. The problem with the presentation approach is that candidates spend all their time talking about what they would do in such-and-such a class rather than actually doing it. That deprives committee members of the opportunity to observe the way candidates present real material in a real-time, quasi-classroom setting. And that's what we need to see in order to hire the best teachers.

Choose a Manageable Topic

While some search committees allow candidates to choose a subject for their demonstration, most panels provide the topic. In fact, committees often give all of the candidates the same topic in an attempt to place everyone on an equal footing. If you don't get to pick your topic, you still have some important choices to make: Exactly what information, and how much, do you hope to convey in the time allotted (usually 15 to 20 minutes)? How will you present it? Will you mostly lecture? Invite some discussion? Involve everyone in a group activity? Dazzle committee members with your technological brilliance?

The first step is to narrow your topic to something you can manage in your few minutes on stage. Here again, one of the biggest mistakes that candidates make is covering too much information—basically, trying to squeeze a 50-minute lecture into a 15-minute presentation. Once again, they end up talking about what they do instead of doing it. My advice is to identify a 15- to 20-minute segment of a familiar lesson, an excerpt that can stand on its own without a lot of background or lead-in material. Preferably, it should be something you've taught often enough that you already know how you're going to present it.

Treat Committee Members Like Students

Sometimes a search committee will give you this directive explicitly, either in written pre-interview instructions or verbally as you're about to begin. But whether they mention it or not, remember that you can't teach without students—and committee members are the only other people in the room. (It's true that a few colleges have job candidates teach actual students in a classroom setting, while committee members observe. But in most hiring situations at 2-year colleges, it's the committee members themselves you'll be "teaching.")

Treating committee members as if they were students means forgetting, for a few minutes, that they hold your professional future in their hands and relating to them as you would to students in a classroom. Address them just as you would address students. Ask them questions, try to engage them in discussion, and call on them to answer. Involve them in activities, whether they, much like real students, appear willing or not.

Although that approach may seem to involve a great deal of role-playing on your part—and perhaps on the part of committee members as well—it actually provides them with invaluable insight into your teaching style, your classroom manner, and your ability to establish a rapport with an audience. Just be careful not to appear condescending. If you do, committee members will wonder if you will treat a bunch of 18- to 20-year-olds the same way, or worse. And don't take the "student/teacher" relationship too far, like the candidate who confiscated a committee member's cell phone during "class."

Do More Than Lecture

Tempting as it might be to stand up and talk for 15 minutes, don't. And for heaven's sake, don't simply read from lecture notes; that's a surefire way to eliminate yourself from contention. At the very least, mix in a little discussion and some question and answer. (One nice thing about having faculty members as your "students:" They're going to know the answers.) And be sure to distribute at least one handout that clearly enhances the lesson.

You might also use a group activity, although I would add three caveats: First, make sure the activity is, shall we say, age-appropriate. Don't be like the candidate who gave each of us on the search committee a cracker, asked us to stare at it for three minutes, and then instructed us to write a paragraph about what we saw. I confess: I just saw a cracker.

Second, don't use an activity that will take up too much of your time. We want you to do more than just lecture, but we do want to hear you lecture. So choose an activity that can be completed in no more than five to seven minutes. Finally, don't expect committee members to be any more enthusiastic about participating in your activity than your actual students would be.

Use Bells And Whistles—In Moderation

After you are invited to an interview that includes a teaching demonstration, one of the first things you should find out is what kind of technology will be available to you. If it's something you're comfortable using—that is, something you already use regularly—plan to use it in your teaching demo. So, for example, if you normally use PowerPoint in your classroom, or like to pull up YouTube videos on the Internet, the committee would probably love to see you do it.

On the other hand, you shouldn't go to great lengths to concoct some "totally wired" lesson plan that doesn't reflect the way you actually teach, just to show how savvy you are. Your lack of comfort (and perhaps familiarity) with the technology will almost certainly be evident. Also, even if you're a bona fide geek, avoid giving a teaching demo that is so technologically based that it's almost a lesson on technology rather than on the topic at hand. Remember, search committees at community colleges are looking for the best teachers, not necessarily the best techies. By all means, dazzle them with technology, but do more than just dazzle. Teach.

And bear in mind that if you do intend to use technology, it's vital to have a backup plan. In my experience, nothing is more common during teaching demonstrations than for the classroom technology to malfunction. So if you're using a CD, have the data on a flash drive as well. Prepare handouts that you can substitute for the images that won't appear on the screen if the projector refuses to boot up. (Here's where those copies of your PowerPoint slides might come in handy.) If all else fails, be prepared to teach in the old-fashioned way.

By following those few simple steps, you can set yourself apart from other candidates. And if you're interviewing at my institution, where I'm once again serving on a search committee, I'm not just suggesting you follow my advice—I'm begging. After all, how many awful teaching demos can one person sit through?

The original essay was published January 16, 2009, in *The Chronicle of Higher Education.*

> The bottom line is that, in any given search, you have a slightly better chance of being hired than you do of inheriting millions from a rich uncle you never knew you had. But only slightly. Just kidding.

WHY YOU DIDN'T GET THE JOB

If another hiring season has come and gone, and you still haven't landed a tenure-track teaching position, you might be starting to wonder if it's just you. Well, it's not. Okay, it might be. To the extent that you engage in Socratic self-discovery, you would know better than I. But the truth is, many of the factors that affect your chances of being hired have nothing to do with you personally.

Before I examine those factors, I should probably issue the following disclaimer: Nothing I say in this column is meant to explain the outcome of any particular search I've been involved with—especially the two I chaired this spring. One of those was a clerical search, the other administrative; both are very different from faculty searches. Instead, I'm writing in general about a process with which I've become exhaustingly familiar over the last 23 years, at five different institutions, as an applicant, a serial committee member, and an administrator.

Internal Candidates

As colleges employ more and more faculty members on contingency contracts, they also create ever deeper pools of "homegrown" talent. These are often people who have taught at an institution for some time, perhaps for years, as part-time adjuncts or lecturers. They may even be full-time instructors, just not on the tenure track. They know the curriculum, they know the culture, they know (and may even be good friends with) members of the tenure-track faculty—including, perhaps, those who serve on the search committee. Most importantly, if their contracts have been renewed year after year, they must have made a positive impression on the department chair and other administrators with influence on the hiring process. It's only natural then, when a tenure-track position becomes available, that some of these folks will be among the front-runners.

If you don't happen to be an internal candidate, there's not much you can do to offset their natural advantage. Perhaps you can take some comfort in the knowledge that being on the inside isn't always an advantage, as colleagues and supervisors who recognize strengths may also be uncomfortably aware of weaknesses. Moreover, although some 2-year colleges feel strongly about promoting from within, many prefer to bring in new faces with fresh ideas, and others are just looking for the best teachers they can get, regardless. (Note: This topic is covered more thoroughly in "Why Adjuncts Have an Edge.")

Personal Agendas

Another dynamic that sometimes exists within hiring committees—and which you have no way of knowing about, much less countering—is that one or more members may have personal agendas. Of course, each member of the committee will bring some sort of bias to the process, as we all do. But some of them may be more attached to their biases than others, and therefore less open-minded. For instance, perhaps someone on the committee has a close friend among the college's long-time adjuncts who is applying. You might think that, under those circumstances, the person ought to recuse himself or herself. But the truth is, if half the people who apply for the job already work in the department, the college can't possibly find enough people who don't know those applicants to form a committee.

Other agendas may have nothing to do with individuals but everything to do with teaching philosophy or political ideology. I've had colleagues in the English department, for instance, who made it very clear that they weren't interested in hiring anyone who didn't share their views on teaching composition. Thus some pretty strong candidates were doomed from the moment they stepped to the whiteboard to begin their teaching demonstrations—and never even knew it.

Committee Infighting

Sometimes, when more than one person on the committee has a clear agenda, those agendas can compete. I've seen a number of committees that were sharply divided, with one member strongly favoring a particular candidate while another backed a different one. If the opponents happened to be senior faculty members or otherwise influential, the rest of the committee members often felt they had to choose sides, usually on the basis of friendship or teaching philosophy. In cases like this, what often happens is that a third candidate emerges as a compromise. Although not the most qualified person in the pool, he or she is eventually offered the job as a way to keep the peace and make everyone on the committee, if not happy, at least less disgruntled.

Administrative Interference

One of the questions that arises during any search is "Who makes the final decision?" At most community colleges, the committee screens the applicants, conducts interviews, and then makes a hiring recommendation which is not binding on the administration but—in theory at least—is given a great deal of weight. Most of the faculty searches I've been involved with followed this pattern, and in most cases our recommendations were implemented. But I do know of situations where committees were told up-front, by administrators, what "type" of person to look for—sometimes with enough detail that it was clear they were talking about a specific individual. I've also seen cases in which an administrator went out of his or her way to block the appointment of a candidate the committee recommended strongly, for reasons known only to that administrator (and guessed at by committee members).

Budget Considerations

We've all known of searches that were withdrawn or aborted due to budget cuts. But even when funding for positions escapes the ax, many colleges these days are still operating on shoestring budgets and may therefore need to take other financial considerations into account. For instance, if an applicant pool is adequately stocked with highly qualified individuals who live close by—such as might be the case when a college employs large numbers of adjuncts—the committee (or the administration) may balk at the idea of paying travel costs for out-of-state applicants. Or the college may want to hire someone with a master's degree instead of a PhD in order to save a few thousand dollars in starting salary, potentially extrapolated and compounded over a 25-year career. Moreover, as many studies have shown, the number of tenure-track positions nationwide is shrinking. That, too, is a budgetary consideration, and it translates into more applicants for each tenure-track job. Which segues neatly into my last point. . . .

Sheer Numbers

The single factor most likely to sink your candidacy is simply that, in today's job market, more and more people are applying for fewer and fewer jobs. As a department chair, I often had to explain this to angry adjuncts who had been passed over in the search process. Some even failed to get an interview. I tried to help them understand that, if 40 of our own adjuncts applied for a tenure-track position, as was common, there was no way we could even interview them all, much less hire them. It's not that they weren't qualified, even outstanding; it's just that, among so many outstanding people, it's very difficult for any one person to stand out. The numbers were simply against them.

The same reasoning applies to people applying from outside the institution. If anything, they may be at more of a disadvantage because they lack the "insider's" edge, assuming such an edge exists. The bottom line is that, in any given search, you have a slightly better chance of being hired than you do of inheriting millions from a rich uncle you never knew you had. But only slightly.

Just kidding. Kind of. I'm supposed to be making you feel better, and I'm failing miserably. But at least if you recognize that the reason you haven't been hired is not that you're genetically unemployable, then perhaps you'll also understand that, with a little persistence (okay, a lot of persistence), you stand a decent chance of landing a full-time teaching position somewhere at some point. That's not a lot of encouragement, I know, but it's the best I can do right now. In the next essay, I'll talk about steps you can take to improve your chances. In the meantime, try to stay away from the hemlock.

Part 4

On the Job as a Community College Instructor

"My computer's hard drive crashed, so I text-messaged you my term paper."

> Beyond merely behaving like a decent human being, one of the best and easiest things you can do to improve your student ratings is to obtain a copy of the evaluation instrument at the beginning of the term and read through it to see what questions it asks.

MEETS EXPECTATIONS

In one of her inimitable columns for *The Chronicle of Higher Education*, Emily Toth (aka Ms. Mentor) poses the question, "Do I hafta publish?" For the majority of readers in her target audience—doctoral students or freshly minted PhDs pursuing appointments at research universities or 4-year colleges—the short answer is yes. But for my primary audience—those newly hired or seeking positions at 2-year colleges—the answer is, for the most part, no. (Whether or not faculty members at community colleges *should* publish is a separate question, and one that I address in another essay. But if the emphasis is on Ms. Mentor's "hafta," then no is the correct answer.)

The obvious next question, then, is, what will you have to do as a faculty member at a 2-year college to keep—and excel at—your job? Like your counterparts at 4-year institutions, you'll probably be evaluated regularly, with those evaluations factoring into decisions regarding continued employment, tenure, and promotion. College systems in some states (like Georgia, where I work) even tie pay raises to annual performance reviews.

The overwhelming majority of 2-year colleges describe themselves as teaching institutions, meaning that teaching (and specifically not research) is their primary mission. Administrators at our colleges, then, judge faculty members largely on how well they perform in the classroom. They may also be evaluated on their service and other "professional activities" (that's generally code for attending conferences and workshops), but teaching effectiveness will always be paramount.

Gauging effective teaching can be a little harder than measuring a stack of publications. That's why 2-year colleges typically use a variety of methods, including self-evaluation (the dreaded "annual report"), supervisor and/or peer reviews (classroom observations), and student evaluations (to the chagrin of many). Of those methods, the one over which you have the most control is the self-evaluation, which usually takes the form of a narrative. In that document, you describe your teaching activities for the past year, placing special emphasis on the assignments, tests, and projects you gave to students and on how you used class time.

In short, the self-evaluation is your chance to spell out exactly what you have done over the past year to help students learn. It should be fairly short—two to three single-spaced pages is plenty. It should be collegial rather than pedantic in tone, and focused more on actual activities than on philosophy (although philosophical comments can be included in order to place the activities in context, as in "Because I believe . . ." or "I frequently have my students . . ."). The narrative also gives you a chance to highlight any new or innovative teaching approaches you might have employed during the past year. (Note that a strategy doesn't necessarily have to be cutting edge to be new to you.)

Administrators at 2-year college are particularly interested lately in any activity involving technology. It may be true that some forms of classroom technology are no better than "gilded chalk," as a colleague of mine used to say, but most experienced faculty members have identified specific applications that are useful to them. Only by trying various approaches can you discover what works and doesn't work in your class-room. If nothing else, your attempts will make excellent fodder for your annual report.

In addition to your narrative and copies of your syllabi, be sure to include examples of assignments, tests, and other handouts that you use in your courses. Your department head may well ask for those documents specifically as part of the evalua-tion process, but even if he or she doesn't, you should attach them. To the extent that you have control over which documents to include, go with those that most clearly support the assertions in your narrative.

Another way that 2-year colleges evaluate teaching is through classroom obser-vation by a peer or a supervisor. If you're a new faculty member, you can almost cer-tainly expect visitors—probably a department head or a dean, but perhaps a veteran colleague—at least for the first semester or two and perhaps well beyond. Those visits may be scheduled in advance or can occur unannounced, depending on the institu-tion's guidelines.

The only way to deal with the uncertainty of an unscheduled visit is to be well prepared for your classes so that you won't panic when your department chairman walks through the door. It's also not a bad idea to develop a variety of extra activities that can be plugged in at a moment's notice to demonstrate your awareness of various learning styles. When that unexpected visitor shows up, just pull one of those activi-ties out of your teacher's bag of tricks and violà, instant good impression.

Finally, if you expect to get good performance reviews, your student evalua-tions must be acceptable, at the very least. Volumes have been written on the subject of student evaluations of teaching, and I won't attempt to rehash that discussion here. Suffice it to say that, for community college instructors, student evaluations are prob-ably always going to be part of the equation. That's just a fact of professional life.

The "secret" to getting good ratings from students isn't really a secret at all, or even much of a mystery—and it doesn't involve giving everyone an A. As an instruc-tor, you can be as demanding as you want, within reason, so long as you are re-spectful to students (no verbal abuse, please, and limit your sarcasm) and consistent in your dealings with them. Treat your students the way you would have liked your professors to treat you.

Beyond merely behaving like a decent human being, one of the best and easiest things you can do to improve your student ratings is to obtain a copy of the evaluation instrument at the beginning of the term and read through it to see what questions it asks. If students are going to evaluate you based on how promptly you return graded assignments, for example, then put a little extra effort into returning assignments promptly. And make sure they understand what "prompt" means (getting their English essays back the next day is usually an unrealistic expectation). If the evaluation form asks students about the relevance of your tests, then take special care to make sure your tests relate directly to the subject matter you have covered, and be sure to point out frequently during lectures and class discussions what sorts of questions you might ask on the tests.

By following those few guidelines, you stand a good chance of being rated highly in the "teaching effectiveness" portion of your annual performance review. Of course, you may also be evaluated based on your service to the institution and on the quality and quantity of your professional development activities. I'll talk about both of those areas in another essay.

References

Toth, E. (2006, March 15). Do I hafta publish? *The Chronicle of Higher Education.*
    Available from http://www.chroniclecareers.com/article/Do-I-Hafta-Publish-/46697/

The original essay was published April 25, 2006, in *The Chronicle of Higher Education.*

> Generally speaking, good teachers get good evaluations and those who consistently receive low marks usually deserve them. The corollary here is that by improving your student evaluations, you can also improve your teaching.

EVALUATE THIS

Quite a few readers took issue with my suggestion, in "Meets Expectations," that it's not really that hard to get good evaluations from students. Always a glutton for punishment, I would like to expand on that idea in this essay. Although my remarks are aimed specifically at new faculty members at 2-year colleges, I believe they apply to other college instructors as well.

From the e-mail messages I received about "Meets Expectations" and from other things I've read, the main complaint regarding student evaluations seems to be that they're capricious. Students don't understand what they ought to value, the argument goes, and so their assessments can't be trusted. They turn the evaluation process into a popularity contest and use evaluations to "stick it" to instructors who are "too hard," even though academic rigor is in the students' best interest.

According to that theory, only "easy" (read: bad) teachers get good evaluations, while "good" (read: hard) teachers are doomed to low marks. An obvious corollary states that the only way to improve your evaluations is by sucking up to students and becoming an easy grader. Based on my experience—including 23 years in the classroom and seven years as a department chair—I would have to say none of those statements is true. In fact, I think the attitudes described above probably say a great deal more about the instructors who hold them than they do about their students. Because let's be honest: Anyone who believes that only "hard" teachers get bad evaluations is probably getting bad evaluations.

As a department chairman, I had the opportunity to review many faculty members' evaluations, observe those instructors in the classroom, see their final grades, and hear firsthand what students had to say about them. From that experience I formed my own hypothesis: Generally speaking, good teachers get good evaluations and those who consistently receive low marks usually deserve them. The corollary here is that by improving your student evaluations, you can also improve your teaching. And my contention is that you *can* improve your evaluations, by following a few simple guidelines.

Remember the Golden Rule

The first key to getting good student evaluations is simply to treat students the way you would want to be treated—or, if you're my age, the way you would want a professor to treat your son or daughter. That means, among other things, that arrogance, condescension, and biting sarcasm should be checked at the classroom door, reserved for department meetings where they belong. I've noticed over the years that the faculty members who complain most bitterly about poor student evaluations are the very ones who regale their long-suffering colleagues each term with stories about their lazy, stupid, ill-prepared students. It's obvious those faculty members have nothing but contempt for students, and it's no mystery why students don't respond to their negativity with positive evaluations.

Balance Justice With Mercy

Some faculty members, in a misguided effort to be tough, adopt all sorts of extreme policies, such as refusing to allow students to make up tests for any reason or penalizing assignments several letter grades for minor infractions. Good teachers understand that there are times to teach students valuable life lessons and times to cut them some slack. Knowing the difference can be difficult, but tough judgment calls come with the job. In the end, students will respect you more if you are willing to listen and take their circumstances into account rather than just blindly adhering to policy, whatever the outcome.

Maintain Your Professionalism

College professors are not Wal-Mart employees, required to stand at the door and greet students with a smile. But we do have an obligation to relate to them in a professional manner. Certainly that involves our demeanor and the way we respond to students verbally. But acting professionally also means that we follow the schedule outlined in the syllabus, weigh grades according to the published scale, and return papers and tests promptly. It means we are prepared for each class meeting and manage class time efficiently. It means we make ourselves available and accessible to students before and after class, as well as during our scheduled office hours. In short, professionalism is at the very heart of what it means to be a good teacher, because it balances the necessary distance with an earnest desire to serve. Students will recognize that and respond favorably to it—much more so, in my experience, than if we try to be their buddies.

Keep It Real

I once received a number of complaints about a young faculty member who was requiring students in her sophomore survey course to write three, 500-word essays in a single 75-minute class period. When I confronted her, she responded by saying she had done it in graduate school and, by golly, those students could do it, too. While that may be an extreme example, I have seen many new instructors, fresh from their advanced studies, attempt to treat freshmen and sophomores like graduate students. Try to remember what your professors expected from you as an undergraduate. Pay close attention to departmental syllabi and common course outlines. Talk to experienced faculty members and ask to see their course materials. Then use that information to develop a reasonable set of standards for making assignments, constructing assessments, and determining grades based on the students who actually populate your classes—not the ones you might wish were there.

It's Not About the A

Most students don't really expect to get As, even though it may seem that way sometimes. What they do expect is that grading will be conducted in a manner that makes sense and seems fair. That means you need to be very clear, in your syllabus and from the first day of class, about what you expect from students and how you will determine grades. Make the entire process as transparent and objective as possible. If your assessment includes subjective elements, such as essays or class presentations, publish your grading criteria beforehand and adhere to them closely. As much as possible, explain to students, through notes or in private conferences, how you arrived at a particular grade. Above all, strictly follow the test schedule and grade distribution outlined in your syllabus. If you don't, you're not just giving your students a reason to "stick it" to you on their evaluations; you're giving them pretty good grounds for a grade appeal.

Be Prepared, and Prepare Your Students

Finally, in order to get the best-possible evaluations, you have to know what kinds of questions students will be asked about you. Before the term begins, familiarize yourself with your college's evaluation instrument. Then let that document influence—to some extent—the way you approach the class.

Several years ago, I noticed some of our best teachers were receiving low marks on an evaluation question having to do with learning outcomes. Deducing that many students simply didn't understand what "learning outcomes" meant, I recommended the instructors add sections called "Expected Learning Outcomes" to their syllabi, talk about those outcomes frequently, and, as they dealt with each one, make a point of marking it off the list. Over time, the faculty members who tried that strategy saw their marks on that question improve, along with their overall scores.

More important, I believe some of them actually did become a little more organized in their approach to teaching and that, over all, students probably did learn more—or at least, understood better what they were learning. So the attempt to boost evaluation scores not only worked, it also helped those faculty members become better teachers. The same would be true for those who resolved to treat students with more respect or become more accessible. Ultimately, the point is that all of us who teach should be working to improve our student evaluations each year. Because, like it or not, evaluations are more than just an annual popularity contest. They're actually a pretty fair reflection of the job we're doing.

The original essay was published November 15, 2006, in *The Chronicle of Higher Education*.

> Helping out in some way in your community—whether it "counts" or not—is an excellent way to build goodwill for your college. (They don't call them "community colleges" for nothing.)

THE SERVICE QUESTION

Besides teaching, what does a faculty member at a 2-year college have to do in order to earn promotion and tenure—or, at the very least, remain employed? In an earlier essay, I talked about the fact that faculty members at community colleges are usually evaluated in three areas: teaching effectiveness, service, and professional development. I focused in that essay on teaching because classroom performance is obviously the most important consideration. But the other two areas play a role in promotion and tenure, too, and often combine to form a significant portion of a faculty member's overall evaluation.

Just as 4-year institutions do, we divide service into two categories: service to the institution and service to the community. Included in the former are those chores expected of faculty members everywhere—committee work, sponsorship of student organizations, and mentoring responsibilities. Typically, faculty members at 2-year colleges are expected (or, at least, encouraged) to take on more of those tasks than their colleagues at research institutions. We don't need a list of impressive publications and conference presentations to stand out; we need evidence of good service.

Let me focus first here on committee work. Serving on some committees is a matter of choice. Service on others requires that you be appointed or elected. Curriculum committees, for example, are usually open to all full-time faculty members who regularly teach in the department or college and want to serve, whereas presidential-search panels are generally filled with appointees. I've always encouraged faculty members new to the tenure track to serve on departmental or collegewide curriculum committees because they give you a good grasp of the pedagogical issues particular to that department or college. They also offer the best opportunity to exert real influence on the curriculum and put your fancy ideas from graduate school into practice—if, that is, you can persuade the old guard on the committee to go along.

Some of the other committees open to any faculty member include those on hospitality, wellness, and special-events planning (like the United Way fund drive or Relay for Life). Membership on such panels will not only fill out the annual report that records your major accomplishments but also can help you make friends at the college and become part of the life of the institution.

The committees to which you must either be appointed or elected include faculty or administrative search committees, presidential task forces on issues such as salaries or workload, and governance committees and policy councils. While appointments and nominations usually go to senior faculty members, junior colleagues who make known their desire to serve may find that wish granted (so be careful what you ask for). Whatever committees you end up on, understand that the term "service" means just that. Some general rules on participation:

- Make a point to attend every meeting, and if you have to miss one, be sure to send the head of the committee an e-mail explaining why.
- Be an active, participating member but not the most vocal person at the table. When asked for your opinion, be honest yet tactful. Behave collegially toward everyone and avoid taking sides too soon—unless you really feel strongly about an issue and are sure you have chosen the right side.
- Volunteer, when appropriate, to lead a subcommittee or take on other tasks on behalf of the group. That way, your committee work can provide more than just short-term annual-report fodder. It can genuinely boost your career by helping you become a respected and influential member of the faculty.

Faculty members can become involved in a variety of other service-oriented activities besides committee work. For example, student organizations—clubs, councils, and honorary sororities or fraternities—are always looking for faculty sponsors and advisers. On many campuses, without a faculty adviser, an organization isn't considered legitimate and therefore can't receive financial support from the college.

Be warned: The job of faculty adviser can be time-consuming. But the payoff is that you get to work directly with students—the main reason you got into this line of work, remember? Also, if you look hard enough you can probably find a group of students with whom you share an interest, like cinema or backpacking. Most important, being the primary contact for Phi Theta Kappa or the College Bowl team automatically elevates your status on the campus.

Another opportunity for full-time faculty members involves serving as a mentor for part-timers. True, some of those part-timers have probably been around longer than you have and don't need "mentoring." But it's also true that most 2-year colleges hire a slew of new adjuncts every year, and those new hires need someone more familiar with the institution than they are in order to help them figure out which documents are due when and to whom, when the copy center is open, where the mailboxes are located, etc.

Even experienced part-time faculty members usually can't be on the campus every day or attend all department meetings, so having a contact just to pass on information is useful. If you're thinking "all of that sounds like the department head's job," think again. Chairmen don't have time, beyond conducting an initial orientation, to shepherd 15 or 20 adjuncts a semester, which is why department heads ask for faculty volunteers.

If you really take the responsibility seriously, you can do more than just pass on information to the part-timers you are advising. An occasional invitation to lunch or coffee probably wouldn't be declined, and could offer an excellent opportunity to discuss pedagogy, teaching philosophy, and other common interests. If you listen well enough, you might even learn something.

Let me touch briefly on the other category of service I mentioned—to the community. As far as your annual report is concerned, that is basically a catchall phrase that includes anything you do outside of your regular work hours for which you don't get paid and which relates, in some way, to your area of expertise. If you are a biology professor and coach your son's Little League team, that doesn't count as service to the community. Judging your son's middle-school science fair, on the other hand, does count.

Helping out in some way in your community—whether it "counts" or not—is an excellent way to build goodwill for your college. (They don't call them "community colleges" for nothing.) At the same time, by moving outside the ivory tower (or the 1960s-style institutional brick shoebox, as the case may be) and using your expertise to benefit schools, churches, and civic organizations, you can increase your own level of prestige within the area and find a great deal of personal fulfillment. "Service to community" might not be the lengthiest or the most impressive section of your annual report, but it may well be the part of the job that gives you the most satisfaction. Except, of course, for your professional development activities, which I'll discuss in another essay.

The original essay was published June 21, 2006, in *The Chronicle of Higher Education*.

> One of the best things about working at a 2-year college is that you don't have to limit yourself to writing about your field . . . You can pursue other academic interests—like my friend the Beowulf scholar who publishes essays on pop culture.

THE OPTION TO PUBLISH

In other essays, I've written about the role of teaching effectiveness and service in evaluating faculty members for tenure at community colleges. I'd like to focus now on the third and final area on which we are assessed: professional development, which may include—but certainly isn't limited to—publishing. I've touched briefly in other essays on the topic of publishing in the 2-year sector and, from e-mail responses, have found it to be surprisingly controversial. Professors at community colleges appear about evenly divided: Some bemoan the fact that they don't have the time or resources to publish, while others worry that they will eventually be required to do so.

Their fear is understandable. At a typical 2-year college, faculty members teach five courses a semester and have mandatory office hours, committee assignments, and other service expectations beyond that. It does seem to be asking a bit much for them to carve out additional time for extensive research and writing. On the other hand, as the academic job market continues to stagnate and community colleges hire more PhDs, another group has emerged on 2-year campuses: faculty members with aggressive research agendas. Considering the potential good those scholars can accomplish for their disciplines, and the prestige that can accrue to a college from having published writers on its faculty, it doesn't make sense either to squelch their enthusiasm or allow it to die from neglect.

The answer, I believe, is for administrators at 2-year colleges to find ways to encourage and support people who want to publish and have the ability to do so. When I say "encourage and support," I'm not talking about a verbal pat on the back at fall convocation or a line in the campus newsletter. I mean that colleges should provide additional money and/or course-release time for those faculty members to pursue their research interests.

My college, for instance, has recently established a fellowship program that uses a competitive application process to identify faculty members with viable writing projects and reward them with significant release time from teaching. The results have been impressive so far, as six fellows representing five disciplines are now at various stages in their book-length manuscripts. Three already have publishing contracts, while two others have received positive responses from academic presses. The sixth, whose project is creative, has had several excerpts published in literary magazines and has attracted interest from agents. (I would be interested in hearing from other readers at other 2-year colleges on how their institutions support faculty members interested in research—or not.)

So faculty members at 2-year colleges clearly *can* publish, and many of them do. Moreover, despite what I said about the influx of PhDs into our colleges, you don't have to hold a doctorate to be engaged in scholarship: Many of my published colleagues are MAs or MFAs. Faculty members just need a little time to do that research and a sense that the college values that work—a sense most easily conveyed through some sort of tangible reward. For those faculty members who aren't interested in doing research, however, there are other ways to satisfy your college's requirement for tenure that you engage in professional development.

One way is to attend conferences and workshops. They can be discipline-specific or focused on pedagogy or technology. They can be local, regional, national, or international in scope, and can be aimed specifically at community college faculty members or open to all interested scholars. Scores of such professional gatherings convene each year, announced via journal ads, mass e-mailings, and fliers posted on department bulletin boards. Suffice it to say that if a faculty member wants to attend a conference or workshop on virtually any topic, there's probably one out there.

Getting to it, however, may pose a problem, as travel budgets at 2-year colleges are usually tight. But most will pay for a faculty member to attend an out-of-town conference at least occasionally, and cheaper options are often available locally, such as in-house workshops or conferences held at nearby 4-year institutions. Faculty members who want to play a more active role at a conference can seek to be on a panel—which means anything from reading an academic paper in the time-honored tradition, complete with nasal monotone, to delivering a slick, Web-enhanced slide show.

A final category I would like to mention under professional development is what some might call quasi-academic or nonacademic writing. One of the best things about working at a 2-year college is that you don't have to limit yourself to writing about your field. Any publication counts. That means you can pursue other academic interests—like my friend the *Beowulf* scholar who publishes essays on pop culture. Or you can write things that aren't specifically academic in nature, such as opinion columns or community newsletters. It's true that professors at research institutions do that sort of thing, too, but for them it's a sideline, a break from their "real work." For those of us at community colleges, such activities reflect our connection to the community and are therefore part of the job.

Ultimately, everything we do as faculty members at 2-year colleges must be viewed through the prism of the community college mission. Whether teaching classes, sitting on committees, attending conferences, or writing articles, faculty members whose primary goal is to serve their communities earn more than just good annual reviews. They also enjoy a lifetime of intellectual stimulation, professional fulfillment, and personal satisfaction. And those are qualities that can't be measured by any evaluation system.

The original essay was published August 14, 2006, in *The Chronicle of Higher Education*.

Clearly it's time for a major teaching makeover, in the spirit of TLC's *Trading Spaces* or, better yet, MTV's *Pimp My Ride*, in which cast members take old cars and update them with new paint jobs, ground effects, stereo systems, and so forth.

PIMP MY COURSE

've always considered myself a pretty good teacher (don't we all?)—a comfortable assumption more or less borne out by two decades of student evaluations. Imagine my dismay, then, when I came across a recent entry on RateMyProfessor.com ripping me as "not a very hard grader" and "pretty boring." I didn't take the first description too seriously, having received numerous end-of-term e-mail messages from students in the same section who clearly disagreed with that assessment. It was the second label that really got to me. "Boring?" Me? No way. I'm too young, too hip, too cool, too cutting edge. OK, would you believe mildly engaging?

The truth is, as far as today's students are concerned, I'm not a "young" professor anymore and haven't been for at least a decade. Nor am I particularly hip or cool. Most days I don't even wear jeans in the classroom, 12 years of administrative duties having decimated my graduate school wardrobe. Worst of all, I'm hardly "cutting edge." To be honest, I'm doing pretty much the same things in class I was doing 20 years ago. For Pete's sake, I still illustrate some of my favorite points by using anecdotes from *M*A*S*H*, that favorite sitcom of my generation that few of my current students have ever heard of, much less watched.

Clearly it's time for a major teaching makeover, in the spirit of TLC's *Trading Spaces* or, better yet, MTV's *Pimp My Ride,* in which cast members take old cars and update them with new paint jobs, ground effects, stereo systems, and so forth. In the end, the cars may be only marginally more functional, but they sure look a lot cooler. Resolving to "pimp my course," then, I went straight to the experts, colleagues who really *are* cutting edge. Under their tutelage, the first thing I learned is that I definitely need to use the computer a lot more during class. And I don't mean just to check my e-mail while the students are writing essays.

Because, as we all know, students love computers. They regard any information that comes to them via computer as being, by definition, more reliable than information from any other source. College professors, on the other hand, are way down the reliability scale. As a teacher, I've got to find a way to harness that "Computer? Sweet!" mentality.

So far I haven't done a very good job. Though not exactly a neo-Luddite, I never fully signed on to the electronic revolution, despite the fact that, like many 2-year colleges, mine is mega-wired, with at least one computer in each classroom. Most also have overhead data projectors, many have Smart Boards or Sympodiums, and a few are even dedicated to computer-assisted instruction, with 24 stations each. I confess that in the past I've grossly underutilized those resources, frittering them away in such pedestrian activities as projecting students' sentences onto the white-board (where I, of course, proceed to rip them to shreds with a red Expo marker) and allowing students to use their computer workstations to edit and revise rough drafts in class (when they aren't looking at MySpace). But there's so much more that can be accomplished with these marvelous devices: captivating Web sites to be visited, live audio and video to be streamed, potent PowerPoint presentations to be projected onto the Smart Board and then read aloud in class. I can hardly wait to begin.

Besides using the computer more in my classroom, the experts tell me that another way to transform my teaching persona is to put more of my course materials online. I can create a course that's more user-friendly and appealing to today's students by incorporating more Web-based elements. That could be as simple as placing my syllabi, lecture notes, and other course materials on my Web site—which would mean that I first have to *get* a Web site. Or, the experts tell me, I could direct students to one of those online tutorials provided by the book publishers, where students can complete additional grammar and sentence-structure exercises. It's true that they don't do the exercises I already assign from the textbook, but I feel confident that, if those exercises were online, students would view them much differently.

To make my "Web content" more dynamic and original, I can record my class-room lectures and link the audio to my site in the form of podcasts, which students can then download into their MP-3 players and listen to while jogging or playing video games. Why any student would actually want to do that is beyond me, especially when it seems they would rather shove bamboo shoots under their fingernails than listen to the live version. But my more-wired colleagues assure me this is the wave of the future (podcasting, that is, not bamboo shoots).

Better yet—and this is definitely one of the coolest new strategies I've come across—I could create my own Internet chat room dedicated solely to a particular class. Colleagues who do that tell me students will say things in a chat room they would never say in class. Given what students do say in class, I'm not sure that's a good thing, but hey, I'm willing to experiment.

But, by far, the best idea anyone has given me is that I should start my own class blog. I've never actually had a blog, but I've read a few, and what strikes me most about them is that the writers—excuse me, bloggers—can say anything they want, apparently without repercussion. In academe alone, we have right-wing kooks, left-wing kooks, anarchists, and openly unapologetic jihadists, each with his or her own blog. Just like my students, there are things I would never, could never, say in class. Clearly, I've got to get myself a blog.

In the end, with a little luck, all this body trim and flashy paint (so to speak) should help make my Honda Civic of a course look more like a street racer. Otherwise, I may just have to try connecting with students using less-sophisticated technology. Better not toss those DVDs of old *M*A*S*H* episodes just yet.

The original essay was published July 11, 2007, in *The Chronicle of Higher Education*.

To the extent that a college really is a business, the type of business it most resembles is a health club.

YOUR FRIENDLY NEIGHBORHOOD INSTRUCTOR

If you want to see a bunch of community college faculty members roll their eyes in unison, just stand up in front of them and utter the words "customer service." At that precise moment, according to a survey conducted informally by me, approximately 67.3% of them will be thinking, "Not again." The other 32.7% are thinking, "For the last time, students are *not* customers."

Either reaction can lead to friction between faculty members and administrators at 2-year colleges. A growing number of the latter group pride themselves on being "business oriented," with a focus on "customers." Meanwhile, the former feel they have been subjected to more meaningless customer-service initiatives than any group of higher education professionals in the country, with the possible exception of instructors at proprietary institutions.

After 20 years as a community college faculty member, I think I can speak for most of my colleagues when I say it's not the "service" part of that thoroughly despised phrase we object to. We all understand that teaching is, at heart, a service profession. That's why most of us got into it in the first place. What bothers us is the suggestion that our students, while sitting in our classrooms, are customers. Because words have meaning, and that particular word carries some pretty dangerous connotations in an educational context.

For one thing, when students hear it, their first association is with that famous if not necessarily correct adage, "The customer is always right." "If I'm a customer," the student thinks, "and the customer is always right, then why am I getting a C in this class?" The next logical step in that thought process is to visit the instructor—followed by the department head and the dean, if necessary—to demand an A, the way any other customer would demand satisfaction at any other place of business.

The other problem with the word *customer*, as applied to students, is its implications for faculty members. To understand what I mean, simply construct an SAT-type analogy: "Professor is to student as [blank] is to customer." How would you fill in that blank? Server? Clerk? Greeter? Is anyone surprised that community college faculty members, with seven-plus years of graduate education, bristle at the comparison?

It's not that college students are *never* customers on a campus. At the registrar's office or when talking to a financial aid counselor, students are customers of a sort, deserving of the same kind of treatment afforded patrons at the Department of Motor Vehicles. (Wait, maybe I should rephrase that.) The point is that the customer–clerk analogy, while it may hold up in other areas of a college, does not adequately describe the relationship between instructors and students. Clearly, students are not always right, nor do faculty members have an obligation to provide satisfaction, if that is defined as giving students the grades they want or expect.

A colleague of mine put it this way: To the extent that a college really is a business, the type of business it most resembles is a health club. People pay to join a health club. In return for their membership fees, health-club patrons can expect use of the facilities and access to expert advice on fitness. But they have not, simply by paying their fees, purchased a right to any particular outcome. Their health and physical condition will improve only as they avail themselves of the opportunity to exercise. Nor have they purchased any particular opinion on the part of the experts in question. The fact that they're paying to be at the health club does not mean a trainer is obliged to tell them their weight is fine when they're carrying an extra 40 pounds.

I like that analogy a great deal but it, too, falls short. For one thing, college professors, on average, are much more highly credentialed than health club personnel. Moreover, the collective membership fees of a health club's patrons really do pay the salaries of its employees. The same is not true at a state college—however much students would like to think so.

At a typical state-supported 2-year college, far less than half the budget comes from tuition dollars. That means the state is really paying our salaries, not individual students (or their parents). It's to the state and its citizens that our real duty lies—a duty to ensure that students can perform college-level work before we award them college degrees, regardless of whether the "customers" like that arrangement or not.

I propose, then, that we reframe the discussion in terms of "professional service," rather than "customer service." After all, that's what we're really talking about, isn't it? Faculty members serving students as professionals? Then perhaps we can identify standards of behavior acceptable to faculty members and administrators alike, while at the same time enabling both groups to achieve their common goals of student recruitment, retention, and academic success.

For example, consider the concept of "friendliness," one of the cornerstones of the customer service movement. That concept does not apply to a classroom setting the same way it might apply in a restaurant or a department store. Faculty members, to do their jobs well, must maintain a certain professional distance. They cannot seek to establish interpersonal relationships with students based on social equality, which is what the term *friendly* implies. In fact, getting too friendly with students can lead to serious problems.

Faculty members do, however, have an obligation to be civil—a human obligation, at least, and I would argue a professional one as well. They should be courteous when addressing students directly. They should strive to avoid inappropriate language. They shouldn't call students names or otherwise belittle them. They should respond with restraint to even the most inane questions—even if the answer is "We went over that in class on Tuesday. I'm sorry you weren't here." None of that has anything to do with "customer service." It's simply a matter of professionalism.

What about the consumer ideal of immediate gratification? Does that concept have any application in an academic setting? To some extent. Certainly, faculty members should return tests and other graded assignments as promptly as possible. When I served as department chairman, students sometimes came to me at midterm to complain that their composition instructors hadn't yet returned any essays. Clearly, that's unacceptable and unprofessional behavior on the part of those instructors.

On the other hand, community college faculty members are not "customer service reps," helping students install computer software or exchange a pair of jeans. They're busy professionals with heavy course loads and numerous assignments to grade, in addition to their other duties. As long as they're returning assignments in a reasonable amount of time—a week or so, in most cases—they're adequately fulfilling their professional obligation. Students, for their part, could benefit from learning a little patience.

In the end, when faculty members hold themselves to the highest standards of professionalism, there can be little question about the fate of the "customer." Because when community college faculty members are anxiously engaged in doing what they do best, everyone involved—student, parent, community member, taxpayer—is well served.

The original essay was published January 13, 2007, in *The Chronicle of Higher Education*.

Perhaps the single most important thing you can do to establish your credibility as a teacher and earn students' confidence is to do what you say you're going to do. Nothing says "rookie" like indecisiveness.

TIPS FOR NEW TEACHERS AT COMMUNITY COLLEGES

The first time I ever taught a college class, nearly 25 years ago, I was convinced that, at any moment, one of my students was going to stand up and expose me as a fraud. Of course, I had good reason to worry: As a brand-new graduate assistant, I *was* a fraud, as Henry Adams has reminded us all in his thought-provoking series of essays for *The Chronicle of Higher Education*, "Academic Bait-and-Switch."

Luckily for me, there was no public denouncement, that first day or any other. Yet even as I finished graduate school and began a full-time teaching career at community colleges, the nagging fear persisted. Only after about 10 years, when I still hadn't been summarily drummed out of the profession (the opening scenes of the old Chuck Connors TV series *Branded* used to play in my head), did I finally start to relax. Perhaps that's why I've always empathized with new faculty members—even when, as an administrator, I've had to supervise and evaluate them. I understand firsthand the anxiety nearly all of them share (whether they admit it or not), and I've observed the different strategies they use to cope. I've also watched as they fail to cope.

Some new teachers, for example, appear timid, indecisive, and apologetic in the classroom, as if to say, "See, I'm not such a bad person. I may not be the greatest teacher, but at least I admit it." Sadly, that strategy usually results in undisciplined classrooms, compromised standards, and artificially high grades. Others come across as arrogant, authoritarian, and patronizing. The fact that they may merely be compensating for feelings of inadequacy doesn't prevent students from growing resentful, complaining to the department head, and writing ugly comments on the student evaluation form (not to mention RateMyProfessors.com). Obviously, the key to succeeding as a first-time instructor at a community college lies in finding the middle path. Since so many seem to have problems identifying that path for themselves, I'd like to offer a road map.

Appear Confident

From the moment you step into the classroom, you must act as though you're in total control and know exactly what you're doing. (Never announce, for instance, "This is my first day" or "I'm kind of new at this.") That your confidence may be entirely feigned is irrelevant, provided you do a good job selling it to students. Remember, good teaching is largely performance theater. If you act confident in your abilities, students will have confidence in your abilities. For you, confidence might not equal competence, but for them it will.

So do whatever it takes to gather your courage. Practice your "I know what I'm doing" face in the mirror. Review the objective evidence that you actually do know what you're doing: degrees, transcripts, CV, shelves of well-thumbed books, teaching contract. If nothing else works, I guess you can always try Stuart Smalley's mantra: "I'm good enough, I'm smart enough, and, doggone it, people *like* me!"

Be Consistent

Perhaps the single most important thing you can do to establish your credibility as a teacher and earn students' confidence is to do what you say you're going to do. Nothing says "rookie" like indecisiveness. Remember that students will try you, especially if they know you're new. They'll beg you to push back test dates, throw out low scores, cancel assignments—anything to make the course less work for them. If they discover you're a soft touch, watch out. They may like you well enough, but they'll have little respect for you. Worse, they won't learn as much as they should.

So determine in advance what you intend to accomplish in the classroom and how best to go about it, borrowing as necessary from experienced colleagues. Know ahead of time which assignments you're going to issue, when you're going to give tests, how much they'll count, and whether you plan to offer extra credit. Publish that information clearly in your syllabus, then stick to it even when students pressure you to change.

If, in the interest of fairness, it becomes necessary to modify the course—perhaps you realize that several test questions were problematic, or you need to spend more time on a particular concept—make that decision objectively and in private. Then present it to the class with a clear explanation of what you're doing (giving a retest, for example), and why. Whatever you do, don't make a change that will create additional work for students. You might as well just lead the entire class down to the department chair's office.

Don't Take Yourself Too Seriously

Few students, if any, are as interested in your subject as you are. Nor are they likely to think it's as important as you think it is. After all, they're probably taking four or five courses, none of them in their major, and each of them taught by an instructor who believes his or her subject is the most important. That doesn't mean your subject isn't important, or that they don't need to learn it. It just means you aren't going to accomplish much by constantly lecturing them on their priorities, or treating every assignment as if it's a matter of life and death. Try lightening up a little. Tell a few jokes at your own expense, or at the expense of your subject matter. Share a conspiratorial wink with students from time to time. They're much more likely to conclude that some aspects of your course really are important if you don't act as if everything is.

Keep Your Distance

Perhaps the most difficult thing in teaching is to establish a user-friendly persona while maintaining an appropriate professional relationship with your students. Some teachers seem to accomplish that effortlessly, but the rest of us have to work at it. Indeed, new teachers usually err on one side or the other: Either they're too distant, which can make them seem cold and arrogant (even if they're not), or else they're too buddy-buddy with their students, which can lead to a different set of problems.

The trick is to be courteous, approachable, and (at times) even self-deprecatory—in short, keeping it real without becoming chummy. To that end, I suggest that you dress like an adult rather than like one of your students. (This is especially important if you're young enough to be mistaken for a student.) Expect students to call you by your formal or professional title—"Dr. So-and-So," "Professor So-and-So," or "Mr./Ms. So-and-So"—rather than your first name. And don't socialize with students outside of the classroom, except during college-sponsored events at which other faculty members are present.

Remember Whom You're Teaching

Always bear in mind that your students are freshmen and sophomores. They're not graduate students or even upper-division undergraduates. For the most part, they're not majoring in your subject. I say that because one of the most common mistakes I've encountered in supervising new teachers (especially those fresh out of graduate school) is that they tend to bring with them the techniques and material they've experienced most recently—that is, in their graduate courses. But those techniques often fail to connect with first- and second-year students when the material is over their heads.

For example, I once supervised a new instructor who expected students in her survey course to write three 500-word essays in a single 75-minute class period. When I confronted her (after half of her students had come by my office to complain), she responded by saying, in essence, that she'd had to do that as a graduate student and, by golly, her students could do it, too. Clearly they couldn't, nor should they have been expected to—not because they were community college students, but because they were sophomores. I'm not talking about watering down the curriculum. What I'm talking about is having realistic expectations and then helping students live up to them.

Despite your initial (and quite understandable) anxiety, following those few steps should help you get your teaching career off to a good start. After that, there's no limit to what you can accomplish—just like your students.

References

Adams, H. (2009, June 16). Academic bait-and-switch. *The Chronicle of Higher Education.* Available from http://chronicle.com/article/academic-bait-and-switch/46949/

Franken, A. (1992). *I'm good enough, I'm smart enough, and doggone it, people like me! Daily affirmations by Stuart Smalley.* New York, NY: Dell.

The original essay was published August 17, 2009, in *The Chronicle of Higher Education.*

> It's especially important for new faculty members to cultivate a good working relationship . . . with the one person who has the most influence over their immediate happiness. No, I'm not talking about the department chair. I mean the department secretary.

THE FIVE CHARACTERISTICS OF SUCCESSFUL NEW FACULTY MEMBERS

No doubt all you brand-new faculty members at 2-year colleges who read my last essay—and probably most who didn't—have gotten off to a strong start in the classroom. After all, teaching is your strong suit. Now you're probably wondering, what about the rest of the job? How do I make the most of those 25 working hours a week (theoretically) that are not spent in front of a whiteboard?

The truth is, when it comes to getting your career off on the right foot, what you do outside the classroom is just as important as what you do inside it, if not more. Certainly you will be formally judged on your teaching, but you will also be judged, both formally and informally, on your performance as a department member and campus citizen. And those judgments will be more public and likelier to stick with you. Based on my own experiences as a "newbie" (four times), as well as my observations as a department chairman and an academic dean, I've identified five characteristics of faculty members whose first few months set a positive tone for their entire careers:

Be Humble

You might be surprised at how many new hires show up believing they're smarter than their colleagues, or thinking they already know more about how the institution ought to function than do people who have been there 20 years. You should assume that, as a rookie, you know nothing about the culture of the institution or the way it runs, much less the way it ought to run. Spend the first few months watching and listening to the people around you, observing how they conduct themselves and how others respond to them. From that you will learn much about how to behave—and how not to.

Seek out an experienced faculty mentor, someone who's been at the college at least three or four years. Avoid members of the "old guard" who appear jaded, disillusioned, and burned out; you don't want their attitudes to rub off on you. Look for someone who knows the ropes but hasn't yet considered using them to hang himself/

herself. (Note: Your department chair may assign you a mentor, but if that relationship is unsatisfactory, feel free to seek out another one on your own. You may very well start with a mentor and end up with a friend.)

Be Willing

I mean willing to do just about anything, within limits. The list of tasks you will be asked to perform as a new hire is virtually endless, as your department head "volunteers" you for various unpleasant assignments (because asking you is less risky than asking someone with more seniority) and harried colleagues seek to shift some of their workload onto you. You will be expected to serve on departmental committees, represent the department on collegewide bodies, sponsor student organizations, judge contests; the list goes on.

Add to those chores the ones that everyone has, like grading exams and advising students, and the load can quickly become daunting. That's why I say "within limits." It's important to be able to say no, especially when all of those other tasks begin to interfere with your primary responsibility of teaching, or leave you with no personal life. But it's equally important to say yes whenever possible, because, quite frankly, that's how you'll endear yourself to colleagues and administrators.

Occasionally I encounter new faculty members who refuse to do anything "extra," anything for which they aren't (in their minds) getting paid. They're determined not to be "exploited" by "the system." The truth is, in a community college setting, I don't even know what constitutes "extra." There's a lot to be done and sometimes no clear delineation between one's official duties and everything else. That's why we expect people to be willing to pitch in and do whatever it takes to serve, well, the system—meaning students, the department, and the institution. If you think that's exploitation, then I suggest you talk with doctors and lawyers about their first-year experiences on the job.

Be Organized

That's the only way anyone can cope with the myriad tasks described above, plus teach five courses, while still maintaining some semblance of sanity. Organization means, first of all, time management. I highly recommend using some sort of daily planner, whether print or electronic. Enter your classes and office hours first, then add other recurring commitments, such as regularly scheduled department or club meetings. Keep track of any new entries as well, including appointments with students, committee meetings, and campus events. Then you can see the gaps in your schedule and plan to use that time for things like grading papers, working on committee assignments, and eating.

Being organized also means keeping track of your paperwork. There's no profession quite like teaching when it comes to generating paper, much of which is vital to the job: class rolls, drop/add slips, course syllabi, tests, handouts. And nothing can be more frustrating, time-consuming, and potentially embarrassing than spending 10 or 15 minutes looking for that one piece of paper you need. So take time to set up a filing system that works well for you. Then follow it. Don't just throw your papers haphazardly across your desk the minute you walk into the office (unless, of course, that happens to be your system).

Be Collegial

Be friendly, open to sharing ideas and materials, and willing to help out a colleague in need. Your collegiality must extend not just to other faculty members but also to everyone else on the campus, including librarians, admissions counselors, and custodians. It's especially important for new faculty members to cultivate a good working relationship—even a friendship, if possible—with the one person who has the most influence over their immediate happiness. No, I'm not talking about the department chair. I mean the department secretary. In fact, that's probably the single best piece of advice I'll give in this column, because having to deal every day with a department secretary who doesn't like you is the definition of misery for a new faculty member. And why wouldn't the department secretary like you? Perhaps because you disregarded my next and final admonition.

Be Low-Maintenance

No one enjoys being around people who are always needy, who always expect others to go out of their way but rarely reciprocate, whose lives are always fraught with some sort of drama. Yet a surprising number of new faculty members fit that profile. (Some not-so-new ones, too.) Remember, while your colleagues might not mind helping you out occasionally, they probably won't like doing it regularly. Department chairs expect to provide a certain amount of mentoring, but they have better things to do than hold your hand for the next 10 months (or 10 years). And, trust me on this, department secretaries divide faculty members into two categories: those who are high-maintenance and those they like.

So make your own copies rather than just leave your handout on the secretary's desk. Don't go to your department chair with a problem you can solve yourself or with a little help from a friend or mentor. Do more favors than you ask for. The reputation you forge during your first year, fair or not, will stay with you at least as long as you're at the college. Maybe longer. It's worth a little extra time and effort (maybe a lot extra) to make sure that reputation is a good one.

The original essay was published September 14, 2009, in *The Chronicle of Higher Education.*

> Keep the doors to the bathrooms unlocked and the lights in the parking lot on until the last lonely scholar has left the building.

ACQUAINTED WITH THE NIGHT

The day I realized I couldn't afford all four of my children, I went to see my department chairwoman. "It's become apparent to me," I told her, "that I can't afford all four of my children. Not on my salary." Her eyes widened. "Does this mean you're quitting?" she asked, with a hint of panic. It was, after all, the middle of a semester, and she could already see herself trying to cover my classes for the duration.

"No," I said, "it means I want you to raise one of my children." Before she could stammer out a reply, I quickly added, "I'm just kidding. What I really wanted to tell you is that I'm planning to start teaching an evening class at [another college a few miles away]. I just wanted to let you know." A few minutes later I left her office with a semiofficial blessing. No doubt she was just relieved she didn't have to replace a faculty member—or take in another mouth to feed.

So began my double life as both a full-time faculty member and an adjunct instructor. For a number of years, while my children were young, I slipped away a couple of nights a week, or sometimes early in the morning, to teach an extra class or two. My wife, also a teacher, had decided early on that she wanted to stay home and raise our kids; supporting her decision meant that I supported the family, too. I needed the money.

I relived that experience recently as I read Professor X's widely disseminated essay, "In the Basement of the Ivory Tower," in the June 2008 issue of the *Atlantic Monthly*. Of all the themes explored in that complex and controversial text, the one that resonated most with me was Professor X's depiction of life as a part-time instructor: the isolation of working evening hours, the sense of being disconnected from the institution. Clearly, Professor X and I have something in common with my favorite poet. "I have been one acquainted with the night," wrote Robert Frost (1928). "I have walked out in rain—and back in rain." Those lines describe my adjunct experience to a T.

Because I needed the extra income to support my family but didn't want to alienate myself from that very family while earning it, I usually accepted classes that met late in the evening, uncomfortably close to what Professor X calls the "graveyard shift." That way I could still make it to my sons' Little League games and my daughter's dance recitals. I could still be a dad. Often the kids were asleep, or at least headed for bed, before I left home for my quasi-clandestine rendezvous with 20 or 25 eager (ahem) students.

I also, on several occasions, taught first thing in the morning, arriving at the crack of dawn, or earlier, to meet a class. That left me plenty of time to get to my "day job." Several semesters—usually in the fall, with Christmas looming—I taught both a late-night class and an early-morning class. That meant, at certain times of the year, I was leaving the building in the dark and arriving the next morning, a few hours later, still in the dark. And not infrequently in the rain.

I often thought about that period in my life after I became a department chairman. Part of that job involved dealing with adjuncts—many of whom had full-time jobs at other institutions—and with faculty members in my own department who were moonlighting for the same reasons as I had. I realized quickly that I was hardly unique. For most of our adjuncts, as was the case for Professor X, teaching in our department was a second or even a third job. We certainly employed our share of "professional adjuncts," scholars cobbling together a living by teaching part time at two or three institutions. But the vast majority had full-time jobs.

Some were on the tenure track at other institutions. Others were stay-at-home moms who saw teaching a couple nights a week as a way of contributing to the family's bottom line while injecting a little sanity into their hectic lives. A few were professionals in other fields who had teaching credentials.

At the same time, I knew several tenured members of my department who were teaching part time elsewhere. Their reasons were familiar: They had young families, their spouses were unemployed or underemployed, their kids needed braces. Between being a moonlighter and supervising them, I learned a couple of important lessons. First, we as full-time faculty members and administrators need to reassess our attitudes toward adjuncts and rethink how we treat them. The sense of isolation that Professor X so eloquently describes, and that I experienced myself as an adjunct, is often palpable in their faces as we pass them—if we pass them—on the way out to our cars.

What can we do differently? A lot of little things. Make sure their classrooms are clean, their dry-erase marker trays well stocked. Stick around a little later than usual one or two nights a semester to drop by their classrooms and introduce ourselves. Keep the doors to the bathrooms unlocked and the lights in the parking lot on until the last lonely scholar has left the building.

And maybe some big things. Make sure they have work space, with computer access, to grade papers, meet with students, and catch up on the day's institutional e-mail messages. Invite them, sincerely, to department meetings and social gatherings. Hold some of those meetings and gatherings at times when most adjuncts can attend.

The other lesson is that administrators need to be open-minded in the way they view outside employment. My current institution, like the one I worked for during my adjunct odyssey, and like most community colleges, has a policy stating that outside employment must be approved, and that it should not constitute a conflict of inter-est. Fair enough. But my experience is that, for whatever reason, most faculty members who moonlight do so surreptitiously, afraid that if they are found out, they'll be forced to quit their extra jobs and maybe even lose their day jobs. Perhaps that's just their own neuroses at work, but I can't help thinking that, because of the blunt wording of the policy manuals and perhaps the attitudes of some administrators, moon-lighters are often made to feel as if they're doing something dishonest and shameful.

I still don't know if my outside employment was ever officially approved. I'm just grateful for a kindhearted, humane department head who understood the position I was in and was at least willing to look the other way. Even if she didn't want to raise any of my kids.

References

Frost, R. (1928). "Acquainted with the night." In *West-running brook*. New York, NY: Henry Holt.

Professor X. (2008, June). In the basement of the ivory tower. *The Atlantic Monthly*. Available from http://www.theatlantic.com/-magazine/archive/2008/06/in-the-basement-of-the-ivory-tower/6810/1/

The original essay was published September 11, 2008, in *The Chronicle of Higher Education*.

> As for guaranteed lifetime employment, well, no one who actually works in higher education believes there is any such thing.

TENURE AND THE TWO-YEAR COLLEGE

The nationwide assault on tenure has found a beachhead, it seems, at community colleges. Of course, not all 2-year colleges and systems have traditionally offered tenure. But even among those that have, the practice is now under attack. Consider the situation in three Southern states.

The chancellor of Alabama's community college system, who stepped down in 2008 to begin a gubernatorial bid, had been accused by faculty groups of seeking to weaken tenure in that system. In Kentucky, the situation is even more serious. Up until 1997, the state's community colleges were part of the University of Kentucky system, and professors could earn tenure in that system. Then the 2-year campuses were merged with the state's technical colleges to create the Kentucky Community and Technical College System. In March of 2009, its board of trustees voted to abolish tenure for new hires, although it didn't revoke tenure for those who already have it. (Update: Responding to the threat of lawsuits and a series of no-confidence votes by faculty members, the Kentucky system's board of trustees voted in September 2009 to reinstate tenure.)

Something similar seems to be happening in my home state of Georgia. We currently have eight 2-year colleges—including my employer, Georgia Perimeter College—that operate as part of the University System of Georgia. Faculty members at those institutions have academic rank and can earn tenure. But Georgia also has 33 technical colleges that form an entirely separate system, and its faculty members don't have academic rank and can't earn tenure. A proposal currently in front of the governor recommends bringing all of the state's 2-year campuses together under the authority of the technical college system. (Interestingly, the committee that drafted the proposal had no representation from the 2-year colleges in the university system.)

Whether or not such a merger will take place, and how it would affect faculty members, we don't yet know. We don't know if our rank and tenure would be revoked, with the inevitable lawsuits to follow, or if we would be "grandfathered in," like our colleagues in Kentucky. But I suspect, along with many other faculty members, that the proposal was motivated, in part, by a growing antipathy toward tenure among certain elected officials. We also suspect that the measure essentially constitutes an opening salvo in the state's war on tenure, which may begin with the 2-year colleges but is unlikely to end there.

If that strategy gains traction nationally, it will be because community college faculty members are fighting the war on two fronts. Not only are we subjected to all the same attacks on tenure from politicians and chamber-of-commerce types as our colleagues at 4-year institutions, but we also find ourselves battling the apathy (at best) of those very colleagues who seem to believe tenure isn't as important at 2-year colleges, or that it somehow isn't as valid for community college faculty members because it isn't as difficult to acquire.

Before I return to that last point, however, let's examine the three most common arguments against tenure raised by elected officials, business leaders, and opponents within higher education: that it exists primarily to protect bad teachers, providing them with guaranteed lifetime employment; that it isn't really necessary, since the Constitution already guarantees freedom of speech; and that tenure has no connection to academic freedom.

The first complaint could come only from someone who hasn't spent a career teaching college students, someone who has merely heard occasional, anecdotal, and probably exaggerated accounts of professorial misconduct. During my 23 years at community colleges, virtually all of the faculty members I've been privileged to work with have been remarkably dedicated and hard-working teachers.

As for guaranteed lifetime employment, well, no one who actually works in higher education believes there is any such thing. We all know that tenure can be revoked for any number of good and proper reasons, such as sexual harassment of students or chronic dereliction of duty. At many institutions, including mine, professors even have to pass periodic performance reviews in order to retain their tenure.

We also know from hard experience that tenure is only as good as the institution that awards it. During the current economic downturn, we've already seen a number of campuses close their doors; tenure clearly did not protect those faculty jobs. And then there are the types of situations mentioned above, where entire systems can morph into something quite different overnight, abandoning the concept of tenure along the way.

The second charge—that tenure isn't necessary because freedom of speech is already guaranteed—shows a clear lack of Constitutional understanding. In reality, the Bill of Rights is binding only upon government in relation to its citizens. It doesn't apply to the corporate employee who criticizes her CEO. Nor does it apply to the college professor who publicly objects to the dean's new program or the chancellor's latest policy. Even though most colleges, as public institutions, are government entities, professors are still "employees" who would serve at the will of their "employers" were it not for tenure.

Indeed, largely because of tenure, a college or university is really not like a corporation at all, as much as some might want it to be. It's really more like a small nation-state, and a democracy at that. (And perhaps that's what the chamber-of-commerce types really find objectionable.)

Just as democracy depends on people's willingness to voice their opinions, so does academe. Faculty members are its citizens, and tenure is their Bill of Rights. Unlike employees of a corporation, faculty members don't merely work for the institution; in a very real sense, they *are* the institution, just as this country is not its government but its people. And, like citizens, faculty members not only have a right to speak out on matters of importance to the whole, but also they are duty-bound to do so—publicly, if necessary. But they can only speak out freely if their livelihoods are protected by tenure.

Which brings us to the final charge: that tenure has nothing to do with academic freedom. To me, nothing could be clearer than the direct connection between the two, especially if we understand academic freedom to encompass not only the speech and actions of individual professors in their classrooms but, more important, the right and responsibility of the faculty as a whole to determine the curriculum. After all, the greatest danger when faculty members are not allowed to speak freely is not that they will lose their jobs—although that is a danger. It's that bureaucrats will ultimately subvert the curriculum for political purposes. (See, e.g., Stombler, 2009.)

Most institutions, including most 2-year colleges, at least pay lip service to the concept of shared governance, the idea that faculty members should have oversight of the curriculum. When that ideal is actually put into practice, it means that lowly assistant professors may find themselves disagreeing with department chairs, deans, vice presidents, and maybe even presidents. And that is as it should be, since faculty members collectively know more about their subject areas than the administrators with whom they sometimes differ.

Faculty members can only speak their minds, however, if they are confident that doing so won't place their jobs at risk should a dean find their remarks offensive. In regard to tenure, that is the precise point where, as they say, "the rubber meets the road." And that's why tenure is just as important at 2-year colleges as it is at 4-year institutions: because it's just as important for faculty members at 2-year colleges to own their curricula. That would be true even without the articulation agreements that allow community college students to transfer to universities with their course work intact. The fact that such agreements are commonplace means that tenure, and faculty control of the curriculum, should be just as important at 2-year colleges as they are at 4-year institutions.

I realize that tenure takes longer to get at most 4-year colleges and universities: six years or more, as opposed to three to five years at the typical 2-year college. No doubt that fact engenders some resentment, even disdain, among faculty members at 4-year institutions who feel that those of us in the community colleges haven't really "earned" our tenure, at least not to the extent that they have. (Even though, by the time we're tenured, we've probably taught as many courses, and more students, in three to five years as they've taught in six or more.)

But what I'm trying to say is that we're all in this together. If our opponents succeed in abolishing tenure at the 2-year-college level, it won't be long before the erosion in skills and knowledge is apparent among students transferring to 4-year institutions—or failing to transfer, as the case may be. According to reports, that's already happening in Kentucky, where transfers have steadily declined over the past 10 years. And once the opposition stands astride the carcass of community college tenure, is there any doubt where it will cast its baleful eye next?

References

Stombler, M. (2009, May 1). In the hot seat. *The Chronicle of Higher Education.* Available from http://www.chroniclecareers.com/article/in-the-hot-seat/44821/

The original essay was published June 11, 2009, in *The Chronicle of Higher Education.*

Part 5

Things to Know About Community College Administration

> Is money the best reason to go into administration?
> Of course not. The best reason is that you're an
> obsessive-compulsive type-A personality. However, as a
> motivator, money is not a bad runner-up.

GETTING INTO ADMINISTRATION

Unless you land an endowed chair or make a mint writing textbooks, administration is where the money is in higher education. That's just as true at 2-year colleges as it is at 4-year ones. Some people might say it's a shame that the best and brightest have to abandon the classroom in order to be adequately compensated. Others would argue that administrators are rarely the best and brightest. But no one can dispute the obvious: Administrators, as a rule, make a lot more money than faculty members.

Is money the best reason to go into administration? Of course not. The best reason is that you're an obsessive-compulsive type-A personality. However, as a motivator, money is not a bad runner-up. But if you're considering a move into administration, you ought to consider a number of factors besides salary. I was a department chairman for seven years and have served for the past nine months as an interim dean, so perhaps my experience will be helpful to those of you about to take the plunge.

The first thing you should know is that administration is hard work. Stanley Fish once said that administrators make more money because "they work harder, they have more work to do, and they actually do it." I don't know that I'd go quite that far. As a full-time instructor, I often taught five sections of freshman composition in a single term, meaning I had about 125 papers to grade every two weeks. I can't honestly say that being a department chairman or dean is more work than that.

It might be more accurate to say that being an administrator is more stressful and carries greater responsibility. There isn't necessarily more to do—in fact, at times I think administrators have less to do than instructors—but what we do is ultimately of greater consequence. That's not to disparage the work of the classroom instructor. But while that instructor may be responsible for one or two hundred students, department heads and deans control the fate of thousands. They have to make sure all the right classes are offered at the right times, that everything is adequately housed and appropriately staffed. If they fall down on the job, the college can't function.

On top of that are the personnel matters—hiring, firing, evaluation, promotion, tenure—for which department heads and deans are largely responsible on most campuses. Botch a few of those decisions and you will come to know the true meaning of misery. Sometimes that happens even when you make the right decision.

And then there's the (often-false) sense of urgency that attends everything a midlevel administrator does. As a professor, I could pace myself throughout the week, perhaps grading 20 papers a day, for instance. As an administrator, I don't have that luxury. When my superiors need something from me, they need it right then.

So being an administrator, if not more labor intensive than teaching, is certainly more stressful. Many capable people never bother making the move into administration for precisely that reason—they don't want the hassle. Others, after a game attempt, simply decide the extra stress is not worth the additional cash. That's something to think about before you apply.

Another thing you need to know is that an administrator's job can be extremely tedious: interminable meetings, multiple and duplicative forms, mind-numbing reports, stacks of documents, endless class schedules, redundant evaluations. (A few months ago my 6-year-old asked me what I do at work. As I patiently described a typical day, I could see that he was growing increasingly disenchanted. Finally he interrupted. "Dad," he asked, "are you a paper pusher?")

Even more tedious, perhaps, than the busy times are the not-so-busy times. In fact, one of the worst things about being an administrator is that I have to be in my office from 8 a.m. to 5 p.m. every day, whether I have anything administrative to do or not. That is, of course, barring all of those meetings, during which I merely wish I were in my office.

I tend to be very efficient when it comes to paperwork, so once in a while, there are days when I have no meetings and finish everything before noon. A professor could simply leave at that point. An administrator can't. You have to sit there until 5 p.m. (with a generous lunch break, to be sure), in case somebody comes by with a complaint. For an administrator, simply being there is a large part of the job.

OK, you're thinking, I could have sworn he mentioned pros in the introduction. Isn't there anything good about being an administrator? Of course there is. Many of the positives are obvious—money, prestige, a degree of control. But some aren't. For example, probably the best thing about being a midlevel administrator, from my perspective, is the opportunity to be an advocate for faculty members: to assist them in their bids for promotion and tenure, to help them find travel money, to be a mentor to those who are new to the profession. Even something as mundane as helping a faculty member move her class into a better-equipped room can be a major source of satisfaction.

Another source of satisfaction lies in knowing that you've played a role in making the college a better place for everyone. Believe it or not, among the long list of committees on which I've served over the years are some that actually performed good and useful work, such as the calendar committee that revamped the summer schedule to create longer breaks or the committee that helped design classrooms for a new building. Of course faculty members can serve on such committees as well, but administrators get to do it more often. With so many committee assignments, some of them are bound to be worthwhile.

Finally, as a department head and dean I've been able to help students in ways I couldn't as a faculty member—for example, by allowing them to register or pay fees or withdraw after a deadline, when circumstances warrant. Of course I can't say "yes" to every request. Indeed sometimes I feel like I say "no" to most of them. But the look on the face of a deserving student when I help him or her out of a tight spot certainly makes me glad I showed up for work that day.

Keeping these pros and cons in mind, I hope you'll consider applying for that chairmanship or deanship when it comes open on your campus, especially if you're an experienced faculty member who's been thinking about making the move for some time. Two-year colleges need good administrators as much as they need good teachers—and the former, in my experience, are much harder to find. And, hey, if you're not a type-A personality, don't worry. Once you get the job, you will be.

References

Fish, S. (2004, November 24). What did you do all day? *The Chronicle of Higher Education.* Available from http://www.chroniclecareers.com/article/What-Did-You-Do-All-Day-/44654/

The original essay was published April 21, 2005, in *The Chronicle of Higher Education.*

Despite the negatives, I still maintain that a good department head makes an invaluable contribution to the institution, and that more faculty members ought to consider taking on the responsibility.

GETTING THE CHAIR

Why is it when a community college faculty member ascends to a position of departmental leadership, hallway scuttlebutt takes on morbid overtones: "Did you hear about Susan? They say she's getting the chair." No doubt that has much to do with the nature of the position. Having been a department head at two different colleges, I can confirm there are certainly moments when you feel as though you've committed a crime—and many other moments when you would like to.

But the dark whispers and death-row jargon have more to do with how the typical faculty member at a 2-year college perceives the department-head position. In my experience, although a few faculty members aspire to the position, most would rather be dead than take the job. I've heard that sentiment expressed repeatedly in my 23 years at community colleges, especially during the years I was a department head: "Who would want that job?" "I don't understand how you do it." "Being department chair is the worst job in the college." Unfortunately, that means many faculty members who would be well qualified to serve in that post, and might actually be good at it, have no interest.

As interim academic dean, I recently oversaw the long-overdue breakup of a large, unwieldy, multidisciplinary department into two pieces, which meant I then had to find someone to lead the new unit. Even with several highly experienced professors in the mix, no one wanted the job. (We finally prevailed upon one of them, but only with the promise that the appointment would be temporary.) While I don't blame any of those faculty members personally, the situation left me scratching my head. At a time when strong leadership at community colleges is most vital—with student demand growing, budgets tightening, and external calls for accountability at their highest—such reluctance on the part of so many good people, though understandable, is nonetheless troubling. What's so bad about the job, anyway?

Personally, of all the things I've done in higher education, serving as chairman remains one of my favorites. It's a position in which one person really can make a great deal of difference, by supporting faculty projects, promoting academic excellence, hiring the best possible people, and helping deserving students. Still, the job definitely has its drawbacks.

To begin with, at many colleges, it really doesn't pay that well in relation to the hours it requires. Although a department head usually has a 12-month contract, that often just translates into a standard 10-month teaching contract prorated for an additional two months. In other words, a faculty member could probably make about as much money, and have a lot more free time, simply by teaching a few summer courses.

Another downside is that you don't have as much freedom as a regular faculty member—freedom to come and go from the department as you please, to work from home, to pursue research and writing interests. A large part of the job is simply being in the office from 8 a.m. to 5 p.m., at the beck and call of anyone who might stop by. Time that isn't spent putting out fires—student complaints, faculty complaints, bookstore issues—is occupied by the position's primary duties: scheduling, staffing, budgeting, and evaluating faculty members. And then, of course, there are the meetings. Lots and lots of meetings.

But what most people seem to like least about the job is that it puts you in an awkward position—directly between the faculty and the administration. Don't be fooled by the organizational chart, which shows straight lines flowing vertically from "academic dean" down to "department head" and then to "faculty." In reality, the vertical line from "academic dean" should be drawn to an inverted triangle, with "department head" at the bottom.

Despite the negatives, I still maintain that a good department head makes an invaluable contribution to the institution, and that more faculty members ought to consider taking on the responsibility. It's not a bad job, so long as you come to grips with certain realities. The first is a clear understanding of your role. Initially, when I became a department head, I thought my job was to keep the faculty, the administration, and the students happy. I soon learned that was impossible. Through a great deal of trial and error, I figured out that the chair's job is actually to keep the faculty happy without ticking off the administration or the students too much.

Presidents, provosts, vice presidents, and even deans are required to take a larger view of matters; they are administrators first and faculty members second, if at all. But a department chair is first and foremost a faculty member—albeit the lead faculty member in the department—and only secondarily an administrator. Of course there will be times when faculty expectations will be unreasonable, or when an individual faculty member will be in the wrong. A wise leader will recognize those situations and take the best interests of the college and the department into account. But initially, at least, the chair's position should be to side with faculty members.

Will that stance make you unpopular with your superiors? It certainly could, if your manner is abrasive or your rhetoric belligerent. But I've found that, generally speaking, if you maintain an attitude of firm yet civil collegiality, and if you show yourself not to be inflexible when the facts do come down against you and the faculty member you're supporting, then administrators will come to respect your position. More important, you will earn the respect and trust of faculty members in your department.

Or most of them, anyway. Because the second harsh reality of department leadership is that some people will not like you, no matter what you do. Certain faculty members will regard you as an administrator, and therefore, the enemy—even if it's apparent that you are consistently a strong advocate for faculty members. A few might be jealous of your position, thinking they could do a better job; heck, some of them might even have applied for your job. And one or two might simply dislike you, for no reason you can discern.

However, you will find that a majority of faculty members in your department will be receptive to your leadership and generally forgiving of your faults, partly because they're nice people, but also because they are relieved that you are in charge instead of them. And you will win over most of the rest if you remember that your first job is to keep them happy without alienating too many students or administrators. Being a department head isn't really a death sentence. At worst, it's life with the possibility of parole.

The original essay was published December 6, 2005, in *The Chronicle of Higher Education.*

> If you want to be known as an administrator who trusts faculty members, throw out the policy manual. OK, maybe you shouldn't literally throw it out; some policies are necessary, after all, like the ones mandating pay raises and vending-machine restocking.

A MATTER OF TRUST

I f you're planning to go into academic administration at a 2-year college, you should probably think about what kind of administrator you're going to be: one who fundamentally trusts faculty members, or one who doesn't. I say that because 23 years at five community colleges, including 12 as a midlevel administrator, have taught me that there are basically only those two types. And although I've had the pleasure of working for, and with, several of the former, the latter certainly seem more common.

Administrators who don't fully trust faculty members are easy to spot. They're the ones whose default response to every situation is to whip out the policy manual, as if it were the sole arbiter of professional conduct. And when an issue arises that isn't covered by a policy, these administrators can usually be counted on to concoct one.

Years ago, I had a department chairwoman who created a policy to address faculty bathroom breaks. (I am not making this up.) The gist of the policy was that, if a faculty member needed to use the facilities during scheduled office hours, he or she had to find a colleague who wasn't currently holding office hours and ask that person to sit in the faculty member's office for a few minutes. I once asked that distinguished chairwoman, during a discussion about hiring substitute teachers for faculty members on leave, if we could hire them to sit in our offices while we went to the bathroom, too. My suggestion was not well received.

Trust-challenged administrators are also notorious micromanagers, which in a community college setting usually takes the form of constantly checking up on faculty members to make sure they're where they're supposed to be. (And not someplace subversive, like the bathroom.) These are the department heads and deans who spend their time roaming the halls, scanning posted office hours, peering into offices, and sauntering by classrooms five minutes before the end of a session.

The worst thing about administrators who don't trust their colleagues, however, is the credence they tend to place in every negative comment or bit of gossip. Such administrators constantly call faculty members on the carpet because a single student (or another faculty member) has made an unsubstantiated complaint—even if the complaint itself is risible or if the faculty member's history at the institution suggests that he or she deserves (at a minimum) the benefit of the doubt. Their attitude: If someone said it, there must be some truth to it.

Such a lack of trust has a devastating effect on faculty morale. And although some administrators apparently don't care about faculty morale, my experience suggests that it's the most important factor in creating a dynamic learning environment, a place where both students and faculty members want to spend time. The question you should ask, then, as a new or prospective 2-year college administrator, is, how can I foster an environment of trust in my department or division, or on campus?

The first step: Recognize that faculty members are highly educated professionals and treat them as such—and not as if they were conscripts or low-wage hourly employees. Don't insult them by constantly checking to make sure they're where they're "supposed" to be. Don't go to their classrooms or offices unless you have a good reason.

If you have problems with specific faculty members consistently not fulfilling their obligations, deal with those individuals directly—and privately. Don't take their behavior as evidence of general laziness on the part of all faculty members. Above all, do not institute policies that penalize everyone just to address the bad behavior of a few.

Speaking of policies, if you want to be known as an administrator who trusts faculty members, throw out the policy manual. OK, maybe you shouldn't literally throw it out; some policies are necessary, after all, like the ones mandating pay raises and vending-machine restocking. But at least recognize that policies are not "one size fits all" and that they are not, in the final analysis, more important than people. To the extent that policies are a necessary part of academic life, do your best to craft and/or support policies that are pro-faculty, that give faculty members more freedom, not less. Whatever you lose in terms of immediate control will be more than offset in the long term by gains in productivity as faculty members feel empowered and morale rises correspondingly.

Another good idea is to be careful how you respond to complaints, gossip, and intradepartmental sniping. Although some complaints, such as those involving charges of sexual harassment, require immediate attention, the vast majority don't. In fact, many complaints from students—regarding grading standards, rigor, fairness, etc.—are baseless and deserve little more than a few moments of quasi-sympathetic head-nodding on your part. The last thing you want to do is start an inquisition every time a student drops by with some petty gripe.

If such complaints are frequent in regard to a particular faculty member, or if they suggest a pattern of unacceptable behavior, then it might be time for you to have a conversation with that individual. Otherwise, assume the best. If you have no reason to believe a faculty member might be guilty of something beyond an isolated complaint, he or she probably isn't guilty.

Departmental gossip and sniping from other faculty members can be treated in much the same way. In fact, you might just want to dispense with the head-nodding and politely tell the sniper you're not interested. But if you choose to let the person vent, remember: Don't believe everything you hear. Your own experiences with a faculty member should weigh more in your judgment than what someone else says about him or her.

Finally, if you want to demonstrate trust for faculty members and earn theirs in return, do everything in your power to support them. Go to bat for them when they're proposing new initiatives that you believe will benefit the college. Nominate them, when they deserve it, for campus, state, and national awards. As much as possible, help them find travel money to attend and present at conferences. After all, becoming an effective 2-year college administrator isn't exactly rocket science. It's just a matter of trust.

The original essay was published October 17, 2007, in *The Chronicle of Higher Education.*

Students might not always like your decisions. OK, they rarely will. But they are more likely to accept them if they know you've actually listened and made your decision based on what you believe is best for everyone involved.

LETTERS FROM JAIL

"Dear Dean Jenkins, How are you? I was told you were the person I needed to talk to about getting a hardship withdrawal. I am currently in the Gwinnett County jail." If you think I made up that letter, you've obviously never been an administrator at a 2-year college. Otherwise you would believe me when I say that not only is that an actual letter but one of several I've received along the same lines. The students who write such letters are seeking to withdraw from classes to avoid getting *F*s on their transcripts, although *F*s may be the least of their problems.

I don't mention those letters to disparage community college students, who are, on the whole, a wonderfully diverse and determined group. I just don't think it makes sense to ignore the reality of who they are and where they come from—and sometimes, where they wind up. I know as an administrator I haven't been able to ignore those realities.

And so as I prepare to leave office after a year as an interim academic dean at a large suburban 2-year college, I want to pass on some of what I've learned about dealing with community college students and their issues. I hope my advice will be useful to others who may one day be receiving their own letters from the county jail.

Try to Be a Human Being, Not a Soulless Institutional Drone
That isn't always easy; after all, you represent the institution, which is, of course, soulless. But if all you do is spout policy and toe the institutional line in every case regardless of the circumstances, what good are you to students—or to the institution, for that matter? The college can program a computer to do that. And the students can just as easily read the policy manual themselves as have you recite it to them. (Which reminds me of a sign I saw a few years ago posted on a faculty bulletin board: "Computers will never replace teachers, but they could very easily replace administrators.")

Part of the problem is that it's always easier to quote policy than to actually make a decision. I sometimes joke with other administrators—those who have a sense of humor, which narrows it down—that you really only need to memorize three phrases in order to be an academic dean:

- "I'm sorry, [insert name of software here] isn't programmed to do that."
- "I'm sorry, that's not my area—you'll have to see the student dean."
- "I'm sorry, that's a [college/state/governing board] policy. There's nothing I can do about it."

Obviously those phrases have their uses. Many times they're true, and sometimes they're all you can really say. But when we routinely use such programmed responses as crutches, or as a means of getting students out of our offices and out of our hair, we're not really doing our jobs. Students come to you expecting human interaction. Give it to them.

Take Time to Listen
One of the best ways to appear human—not to mention humane—is actually to listen. Students come equipped with an awe-inspiring variety of stories about car accidents, drunken-driving arrests, deaths in the family, altered work schedules, drive-by shootings (I'm not kidding), unexpected pregnancies, expected pregnancies, instructor misconduct—the list goes on. Some of them will be in tears. (That reminds me, I almost forgot the most important tip for new administrators: Always keep an open box of Kleenex on your desk, with several more in reserve.)

A surprising number of those students simply want someone to listen to them. Often, by the time they get to me they've already been to several other offices and have yet to fully tell their story. People keep cutting them off as soon as it becomes apparent they can't help—which I understand, on one level. People in some offices hear a lot of stories, and out of self-preservation they're forced to engage in some sort of triage. Many times the snap diagnosis is, "You'll have to talk to the dean."

This year, that's been me. A large part of my job is simply sitting there and listening while students talk. Sometimes that's all they want. Mostly it's not. Mostly they want something from me, and many times I have had to say no. But I rarely have a student leave my office who doesn't feel a little better just for having said what was on his or her mind.

Temper Mercy With Wisdom
The problem with listening to students' heart-wrenching stories is that, at the end, you naturally want to help. And it may well be within your power as dean or department chair to help—to allow a student to enroll in a full section or to register late or to withdraw after the deadline. In some cases those actions might be justified. But most of the time, I've found (soulless institutional drone that I am), it's better to stick to the policy. After all, those policies exist not to make students' lives miserable, as they often suspect, but to promote the greater good—at least in theory. If you find that that's not the case with a particular policy, then work within the system to change it. But most of the time policies exist because they make the processes of enrollment, registration, grading, and so forth run smoother for everyone.

How do you know when to stick to policy and when to make an exception? To answer that, I always ask myself two questions:

- What are the long-term ramifications of the decision for the student, for my colleagues, and for the institution?
- Is this decision fair not only to this student but to other students?
- Many times what seems to the student like the answer to all his or her problems in actuality only creates more problems.

For example, say you allow a student to enroll in a difficult course 10 days late because he or she was involved in a complicated family situation and unable to register on time. The truth is, that student may well be so far behind that catching up is next to impossible; and the student, who seemed so relieved when you made the exception, may later come to regret his or her decision—and yours.

Then there's the impact of your decision on the faculty member and the other students in the class. Is the instructor expected to take time out of his or her already tight schedule to bring the latecomer up to speed? Must the other students sit idly while the class backtracks for two or three days? And how about the issue of fairness? Is it fair to the student to subject him or her to that kind of pressure? Is it fair to other students who wanted to register late but were simply out of luck? (Perhaps you even told a few of them no yourself.)

In the end, listening to students and responding humanely to their issues doesn't mean that you have to be a pushover. Sometimes, when it's in the best interests of the student and doesn't harm the institution, and when it's within your power to do so, you may choose, out of compassion, to make an exception to policy. Other times, the truly compassionate choice—the one that best serves everyone's interests—will be to deny the student's request, as gently as possible.

Students might not always like your decisions. OK, they rarely will. But they are more likely to accept them if they know you've actually listened and made your decision based on what you believe is best for everyone involved. One day, some of those students might even come to appreciate what you did. And if nothing else, you can always visit them on Sunday afternoons.

The original essay was published June 29, 2005, in *The Chronicle of Higher Education*.

> Our obligation . . . is to act in students' best interests, which sometimes means letting them suffer the consequences of their irresponsible behavior—procrastination, laziness, poor study habits—rather than allowing them to shift the blame onto their professors.

"MY TEACHER DOESN'T LIKE ME"

took some heat for writing, in "A Matter of Trust," that "many complaints from students . . . are baseless." One e-mail correspondent accused me of making "sweeping generalizations." Another insisted that since I had made the remark in an essay for *The Chronicle of Higher Education's* "The Two-Year Track" segment, I was singling out community college students, "the vast majority [of whom] do not have time to create baseless complaints and follow up with administrators, deans, and department chairs about them."

Of course, I never said, "Many 2-year college students make baseless complaints." I said, "Many complaints are baseless." There's a huge difference. It's true that the majority of community college students rarely complain, even when they should. Complainers constitute a small minority. And yet they are a vocal and persistent minority. In fact, students with complaints about faculty members—baseless or otherwise—take up a great deal of a typical department head's day. Deans and other senior administrators end up seeing some of those students, too, but when it comes to dealing with complaints, the chairs are on the front lines.

During my seven years as a department chairman, I supervised close to 200 full-time and part-time faculty members, most of them excellent teachers. And yet I can honestly say that I received complaints about every single one. At least 70% of those complaints were of the "my teacher doesn't like me" variety from students convinced that their own failings were actually their professors' fault. This category also includes gripes about grading standards ("I don't understand why this essay got a *C*"), fairness ("I think she has a bias against men"), and rigor ("He expects us to do way too much reading"). Let me be clear: Students have a right to complain and deserve to be heard. But beyond that, the chairman's job is to determine whether the complaint is valid and then deal with it accordingly.

Here's the procedure I developed for handling student complaints—one I would recommend to new or prospective department heads: First, I would ask if the student had talked to the professor about the perceived problem. If the answer was "no," I would politely end the discussion by suggesting that the student take up the issue with the professor directly. Rarely would I see that student back in my office to follow up on the same complaint. If a student had talked to the professor about the problem but was still unsatisfied, then my approach was to listen carefully to the complaint to see if I could detect any hint of validity. If not, I would make vaguely sympathetic noises at appropriate intervals and ultimately suggest some positive course of action, such as going to the writing lab, forming a study group, or not logging onto Facebook during class.

Obviously, my judgment in those cases was often influenced by what I already knew of the faculty members in question. For example, a student once came to me claiming that her humanities professor had a personal vendetta against her. In the student's estimation, the low grades she had received on several tests constituted proof positive. Unfortunately for the student, her professor was one of the most highly respected people on the campus, admired (as her classroom evaluations showed) by students and colleagues alike. I had visited her classroom on more than one occasion and knew firsthand of her teaching ability and professionalism.

Rather than jumping to the conclusion that this esteemed co-worker must have some sinister personality flaw that no one had ever noticed, I recognized the student's complaint for what it was: sour grapes. I listened to her, thanked her for coming, politely suggested she apply herself a bit more vigorously to her studies, and showed her to the door.

Admittedly, on a few occasions, prior knowledge of faculty members has influenced my judgment in the opposite direction. For example, when several students complained that their professor was using inordinate amounts of class time to espouse bizarre conspiracy theories, I had no problem believing them—having been buttonholed more than once myself by that same professor espousing those same theories. Soon after, he and I had a frank discussion about appropriate subject matter for the classroom.

I've also been influenced, in a number of cases, by the complaining students themselves. Some of them I knew beforehand, while others simply impressed me with their sincerity. And sometimes the sheer volume of complaints cannot be ignored. Several years ago my department hired a young faculty member who interviewed extremely well and came to us highly recommended. Yet within a few weeks I began hearing complaints about her tests. According to the students coming by my office, she would assign them to write three 500-word essays during a one-hour test period. Several of the complainants were former students of mine who had done well in my courses and who had high GPAs. All of them were failing her class. When I spoke to the faculty member, she confirmed what the students had said but expressed her belief that "they were college students" and "ought to be able to handle it." So we talked, and I shared with her my experiences teaching sophomore survey courses as well as a few thoughts regarding realistic expectations.

Such examples, however, are the exception. The majority of student complaints turn out to be baseless. Department heads who follow up each gripe with a CSI-worthy investigation will find themselves overworked and unpopular, while trying to explain to their superiors why faculty morale and department productivity continue to decline. Effective chairs, on the other hand, deal with each complaint as common sense dictates—which, about 70% of the time, means ignoring it.

That is not, as my e-mail correspondents might argue, an antistudent position. On the contrary, our obligation as higher education professionals is to act in students' best interests, which sometimes means letting them suffer the consequences of their irresponsible behavior—procrastination, laziness, poor study habits—rather than allowing them to shift the blame onto their professors. Bailing students out in those situations doesn't do them any good and, in fact, may do them a great deal of harm.

And if taking such a practical approach to student complaints means that a department head gets labeled "profaculty," well then, so much the better. After all, my experience has clearly shown that, in disputes with students, faculty members are usually in the right. Not to make a sweeping generalization or anything.

The original essay was published May 20, 2008, in *The Chronicle of Higher Education.*

> Like cats, professors tend to be highly intelligent, deeply self-actualized, and fiercely independent.

HOW ARE PROFESSORS LIKE CATS? LET ME COUNT THE WAYS

I haven't always been a cat person. For much of my life I preferred dogs, which are more inclined to show affection, express appreciation, and come when called. In other words, when it came to pets, I was a narcissistic control freak. Then my family adopted a large tabby named Peanut Butter from some friends who were moving and couldn't take him along. At first my relationship with this proud feline was strained, but I soon found myself admiring his independent spirit and graceful insouciance. Over time Peanut Butter and I developed what I would describe as a good working relationship: I provided him with food, water, and a warm place to sleep, and, in return, he would occasionally climb up on my lap and allow me to scratch his ears.

Perhaps that's why I was so intrigued the first time I heard the term "herding cats" in reference to managing faculty members. That was several years ago, when I was getting ready to start a new job as a department chair. About a week before I was slated to report for duty, I got a call from the departing chair inviting me to lunch. She was leaving on good terms and felt a duty to fill me in on the department and its personalities. Predictably enough, we ended up talking mostly about the personalities, of which (it turned out) the department had quite a few. It was obvious that, while my host held her colleagues in high esteem, she also found them to be frustratingly independent at times. Toward the end of our conversation, she laughed and said, "Some days this job is like herding cats."

In the years since that lunch date, the "faculty are like cats" analogy has become a cliché. But just like "hard as nails" and "dark as night," it has attained that status precisely because it's so ridiculously self-evident. How are college faculty members like cats? Let me count the ways.

Like cats, professors tend to be highly intelligent, deeply self-actualized, and fiercely independent. They need to be stroked occasionally, but only on their own terms and in their own good time. Mostly, they just want to be left alone to do their own thing. They might not come when called—perhaps because they're suspicious of the caller's motives—but they may very well show up on their own when least expected. In fact, the real question isn't whether or not faculty members are like cats. The real question is, "What's wrong with that?" Perhaps, instead of constantly trying to rein in faculty members, we should be cultivating their catlike qualities.

Take independence. It's true that many faculty members, perhaps most of them, seem to view themselves as independent contractors rather than employees in the traditional sense. They sometimes find themselves at odds with administrators who definitely regard them as employees, in every sense. For college professors, however, independent-mindedness is hardly a negative trait. Indeed, it's largely responsible for the rich diversity of personal viewpoints, teaching approaches, and classroom methodologies that makes getting a college education such a rewarding experience.

Another quality I admire in cats is that they have a certain moral integrity. The truth about dogs is they can be bought. Cats generally can't. You won't see anybody bribing a cat with a kitty treat. Oh, it might take the treat, but it will still do exactly as it pleases. Similarly, good faculty members are not easily manipulated—much to the frustration of some administrators, who think they can persuade professors to embrace the latest make-work mandate simply by stroking them with vague promises, empty rhetoric, and meaningless awards. Like cats, professors are naturally suspicious, not because they're cynical (although some are) but because they're highly sensitive to ulterior motives.

Clearly, the real problem with the phrase "herding cats" isn't the "cats" part; it's the idea of "herding." Whenever I hear an administrator resort to that metaphor, I just want to ask, "Then why don't you quit trying to herd them?" Of course, we all know the answer to that question. It's covered thoroughly in Michael C. Munger's (2010) excellent essay on good administrators, "The Right Kind of Nothing," which offers some of the best insight into administrative behavior I've ever read. Munger says that administrators can basically be categorized by the degree of control they seek and the amount of responsibility they accept. Sadly, many want a great deal of control but aren't willing to accept much responsibility—and even some who do accept responsibility still crave control. It's those administrators—the control freaks—who are so determined to ride herd on the faculty cats.

Anyone who's been a college administrator at any level knows that, occasionally, you do have to get faculty members all moving in the same direction. You might have to do that for the purpose of putting together an accreditation report, perhaps, or a curriculum review, or simply using the copier less because your budget has been slashed yet again. Good administrators, however, recognize that the way to mobilize faculty members is not by attempting to push them in a direction in which they don't want to go.

Instead, you must first ensure that you're consistently meeting their basic needs and that you're not trying to make their jobs needlessly difficult. Then you appeal to their reason, using logic and facts. That's much harder than handing out treats but will yield better results in the long run. Because if what you want faculty members to do is actually good for the department or the college, and if you can make a good case for it, then the majority will usually go along. (The corollary is that, if you can't get a majority to go along, then what you want probably isn't good for the department or the college.)

In the end, as an administrator, you'll experience only frustration if you persist in thinking of faculty members as stubborn felines who must constantly be prodded. Just feed them regularly, don't abuse them, don't patronize them, and occasionally they might climb up on your lap and purr—metaphorically speaking, of course.

References

Munger, M. C. (2010, January 7). The right kind of nothing. *The Chronicle of Higher Education*. Available from http://www.chroniclecareers.com/article/the-right-kind-of-nothing/63344/

The original essay was published April 12, 2010, in *The Chronicle of Higher Education*.

"A GREAT MAN, DUMBLEDORE"

Anticipating the release of the sixth *Harry Potter* movie in July 2009, I spent much of the preceding spring rereading all seven volumes of the popular series. (Mixed in with the usual Proust and Kierkegaard, of course.) Taking them one after another, rather than waiting a year between installments, gave me a new perspective on the novels and provided some interesting insights—not the least of which is that Albus Dumbledore, headmaster of Hogwarts School of Witchcraft and Wizardry, might just be the greatest academic administrator of all time.

Indeed, in her books, J. K. Rowling covers the entire spectrum of administrative types, giving us not only Dumbledore but also his antithesis: the petty, vindictive, rule-mongering bureaucrat cum professor, Dolores Umbridge. Since I can find no evidence that Rowling ever worked at an American community college, I can only conclude that administrators are much the same the world over. The truth is, while I've known a few administrators who were Dumbledore-esque, I've also seen my share of Umbridges. Most campus officials, frankly, fall somewhere in between, but I like to think that a heartening number have Dumbledorean potential.

So what is it, exactly, that makes Hogwarts' headmaster such an exemplary leader? And what can 2-year college administrators learn from him? The first and most important lesson has to do with trust. The key to good leadership is to earn people's trust —which generally means trusting them first. That is something that Dumbledore does consistently and conspicuously. Consider his treatment of Hagrid, Hogwarts' giant gamekeeper, whom Dumbledore hired after he was expelled from the school for something he didn't do. Many in the "wizarding community" seem to regard the admittedly uncouth half-giant as something of an oaf, if not a borderline monster. But Dumbledore never loses faith in Hagrid, ultimately appointing him to the faculty. And it is Hagrid, in turn, who utters the pronouncement that I borrowed for my title.

Even more noteworthy is Dumbledore's trust in Snape, the oily potions master whom nearly everyone else suspects of being in league with the dark wizard, Lord Voldemort. Once again, Dumbledore never wavers. When others confront him with what they consider evidence of Snape's treachery, the headmaster always has the same answer: "I trust Severus Snape." It's worth noting (spoiler alert) that Dumbledore is right to trust both Hagrid and Snape, and that, in the end, his faith in them is repaid many times over. Like any good academic administrator, he knows his faculty well, knows whom he can trust, and isn't afraid to bestow that trust.

Not only does Dumbledore trust his faculty members, he consistently has their backs —even to the point of putting himself in jeopardy. For example, a student's accidental injury in Hagrid's "Care of Magical Creatures" class leads some parents to call for the gamekeeper's dismissal, especially after the victim shamelessly plays up the minor incident. But Dumbledore will have none of it, even standing up to the state legislature —I mean, the Ministry of Magic —on Hagrid's behalf.

On another occasion, Umbridge, who has managed to acquire the title of High Inquisitor (which I take to be something like a dean), not only dismisses the school's divination teacher, Professor Trelawney, but orders her to leave Hogwarts at once. The poor woman is devastated, having no place else to go. Enter Dumbledore, who countermands Umbridge's edict and allows Trelawney to stay. He knows well that his intervention might cost him his own position—and indeed, he is temporarily removed as headmaster later in the story—but he's willing to take that risk to support a faculty member.

Dumbledore also does the one thing the faculty members value perhaps even more than administrative support: He leaves them alone and allows them to do their jobs. In other words, to use the modern term, he's not a micromanager. In fact, for long passages he disappears from the narrative altogether, while professors Snape, McGonagall, Sprout, Flitwick, et al., carry on, essentially unsupervised, with the important business of teaching students.

For an administrator, resisting the urge to meddle requires a great deal of confidence, not only in one's colleagues but in one's own judgment. It's also the hallmark of great administrators everywhere, who hire the best people they can, put them in positions to be successful, and then get out of their way. Note that, during those times when Dumbledore is rarely seen in the narrative, the school still manages to function just fine, barring occasional attacks by three-headed dogs, giant snakes, or assorted other horrific monsters.

While he generally leaves the business of education up to the faculty, Dumbledore, like all good administrators, does not shy away from making tough decisions when necessary. It is he, for instance, who decides, over the objections of some faculty members and parents, that the school should remain open even after four students are petrified by a basilisk (which I take to be something like a provost). Dumbledore also allows Harry to compete in the Triwizard Tournament, despite the fact that he doesn't meet the age requirement and the knowledge that Harry's inclusion will anger the other schools involved in the competition.

It hardly needs to be said that those decisions, like most of Dumbledore's, turn out to be the right ones: The basilisk is destroyed, Harry wins the tournament, and Voldemort's evil plot to regain power is uncovered. We're talking about works of fiction, after all. In real life, not every decision an administrator makes ends up saving the world. Some might even be wrong. But great administrators have the courage to make those risky decisions, nevertheless.

Of course, even Dumbledore is wrong sometimes—and, like all great administrators (and great individuals of any stripe), he isn't afraid to acknowledge it. In *The Half-Blood Prince,* for instance, he tells Harry, "I make mistakes like the next man. In fact, being—forgive me—rather cleverer than most men, my mistakes tend to be correspondingly huger" (Rowling, 2005). Later he apologizes to Harry directly for holding back information in an attempt to protect him. That is an important lesson for anyone who thinks that being in charge means never having to say you're sorry. Actually, quite the opposite is true. A good administrator must frequently admit to being in the wrong, sometimes even when he or she actually isn't.

Finally, my favorite thing about Dumbledore—and perhaps the rarest of qualities in an administrator—is his eternal good humor and civility. During the confrontation with Umbridge that I mentioned above, while the High Inquisitor is ranting and fuming, Dumbledore remains unflappable, smiling, even. In fact, I can't think of a single instance in any of the books when he raises his voice in anger. Even as the Death Eaters approach to take his life, he remains civil to the end: "'Good evening, Amycus,' said Dumbledore calmly, as though welcoming the man to a tea party. 'And you've brought Alecto too … Charming … The woman gave an angry little titter. 'Think your little jokes will help you on your deathbed then?' she jeered. 'Jokes? No, no, these are manners,' replied Dumbledore" (Rowling, 2005). Now there's a great administrator for you: someone who can stare disaster in the face and meet it with equanimity.

Of course, not everybody can be a Dumbledore, but 2-year college administrators can certainly benefit from his example. At the very least, they can learn to resist their more Umbridge-like urges, and thus save a herd of angry Centaurs (which I take to be something like a faculty senate) the trouble of carrying them off into the Forbidden Forest.

References

Rowling, J. K. (2005). *Harry Potter and the half-blood prince.* New York, NY: Scholastic.

The original essay was published June 21, 2009, in *The Chronicle of Higher Education.*

> Back then I argued not against distance learning . . . but at least for a more measured approach . . . My arguments were brushed aside like those of a talk-show guest in a policy debate.

A TECHNOPHOBE'S GUIDE TO MANAGING ONLINE COURSES

True confession: I've never been a big fan of online courses. My favorite thing about teaching has always been the direct interaction with students and the energy that it generates—what some might call the "performance aspect" of teaching. I'm not sure how that translates over the Internet. And no, before you ask, I've never taught online. I've never gone bungee jumping, either, but I'm pretty sure I wouldn't like it.

Moreover, professionally speaking, I've always been a little skeptical of Web-based classes. It's difficult for me to comprehend how so many vital aspects of teaching and learning—lectures, class discussions, hands-on demonstrations, synergy among students—can be fully recreated in a virtual environment. After all, doesn't "virtual" mean "not quite"? On the other hand, when I was a department head, no one above me on the organizational chart ever asked me what I thought about online courses. I was just told to put them on the schedule.

I became a chair in the mid-1990s, at the onset of what we might call the online revolution. Back then I argued not against distance learning—that would have been career suicide—but at least for a more measured approach, as my campus (like every other) raced to offer more and more online courses, mostly for financial, not pedagogical, reasons. My arguments were brushed aside like those of a talk-show guest in a policy debate. Within a few years I found myself operating professionally in a brave new world, one in which the number of online courses offered by faculty members in my department alone seemed to double each year. It was a world not of my own making, but one in which I was expected not only to function but lead.

Since then I've learned a great deal, not the least of which is that I might have been wrong about online courses. Oh, I still have no interest in teaching them myself, and I still believe some administrators see distance learning as a cash cow without much regard for quality. But as some of the people I respect most in the profession have embraced online teaching, I've had to reconsider my preconceived notions. Maybe, as my colleagues tell me, you really can recreate the most important aspects of the classroom experience in a virtual environment. Perhaps, as they insist, that environment even has certain advantages over face-to-face interaction. Regardless, online classes are clearly here to stay, at least until they're replaced by ... what? Holograms? Vulcan mind melding? Who knows.

That's one of the hard truths I've had to accept as an academic administrator who is, in some respects, a bit of a neo-Luddite. Another is that, whatever I might think of online courses, they are loved by lots of students. And even some who might not love such courses end up taking them anyway for personal reasons, such as the fact that those students are in Afghanistan. That is especially true at community colleges, where our students must juggle course work with jobs and families. For many, online classes are a godsend.

Faced with those realities, and notwithstanding my mild technophobia, I struggled to become a good and conscientious department chair for my faculty members who taught online. For any administrators who find themselves in a similar position—and I suspect there are many—I offer the following suggestions.

Suspend Your Skepticism

Maybe you're like me: You can't see yourself ever even taking an online course, much less teaching one. Maybe you're secretly (or not so secretly) doubtful as to whether those courses are as good as the face-to-face versions. As an administrator, you have two choices. You can either resign in protest or resolve to make sure your department offers the best online courses possible. If you choose the latter, you have an obligation to treat those courses (and the faculty members who teach them) just like any others, and not like stepchildren. Along the way you may well discover, as I did, that many of your assumptions are incorrect and your suspicions largely unfounded.

For example, a common assumption among administrators is that teaching online somehow requires less effort than teaching face-to-face, and that faculty members who teach "at a distance" are just trying to get out of work. They just want to lounge around the house in their pajamas while the rest of us go to the office. My experience working directly with online faculty members suggests that teaching a course on the Web actually requires more time and effort than teaching it in a traditional classroom. And yes, some of those professors may very well be working in their PJs—at 2 a.m., when administrators are fast asleep.

Support Your Professors

You might not know much about teaching online or care much for the idea, but you have people in your department who do. No doubt some of them are among your best faculty members. Trust their judgment. Defer to them in matters that involve distance learning. Go to bat for them with the administration when they want to offer new online courses or have ideas about better ways to do things—just as you would go to bat for any faculty member pursuing a worthwhile endeavor.

A few years ago, a colleague who had been one of the pioneers of online delivery at our college—and who was universally recognized as being very good at it—decided she wanted to teach her entire load online. At the time, that was against college policy. (Although I never could find that policy in writing. Odd.) As her chair, however, I saw no reason she shouldn't do it and every reason she should—student demand was certainly there—so I approved her request.

The next day the dean showed up in my office, demanding to know why I had allowed that faculty member to flout (unwritten) policy. I told him we had five online sections—already full of students—that needed to be taught, and that we could either allow her to teach all five, thereby making her happy and providing students with an excellent instructor, or we could demand (per "policy") that she teach two of her classes face-to-face and then twist somebody else's arm to cover the remaining online sections, thus creating unhappiness all around—especially, perhaps, among students. The dean harrumphed (yes, he literally harrumphed), and said, "Well, it's your department," and strode out the door. Not only has that colleague been teaching her entire course load online ever since, but the college now has a large cadre of faculty members who do the same.

Learn All You Can

The fact that you're not an expert about online pedagogy, or that you don't have any personal interest in the subject, doesn't mean you can't at least learn the basics of how courses are taught online. I'm sure your college, like mine, offers numerous training seminars for those who want to teach online. You might not have time to attend all of those sessions—nor do you need to—but you can probably fit in at least a few. You also have a great resource in your online instructors. Most of them will be happy to give you access to their courses and perhaps even walk you through them. The IT experts on your campus can also help out and answer your questions. So don't be afraid to ask.

You can even learn from students. They'll be happy to tell you who are the best (and worst) online instructors. Of course, you can't always take what they say at face value, because much of it will be sour grapes and petty complaints along the lines of, "He makes us read too much" or "I don't think she likes men." But over time, if you listen to students, you can certainly detect patterns and trends that may inform some of your managerial decisions.

Just Relax

No one expects you to know everything about every aspect of your department, especially if you lead one of those multidisciplinary megadepartments so common on community college campuses. As a chair, I supervised faculty members in drama, speech, reading, and art—none of which is directly related to my field, English. My good friend the physicist chaired a department full of biologists, chemists, and environmental scientists. And so it goes.

Once you learn to look at online teaching as a type of specialization, you can place it in its proper perspective. Your primary role as an academic leader is to maintain the quality of your department's course offerings, online or otherwise. You don't have to know all the ins and outs of the technology, and you don't need to have taught online yourself, to judge whether or not an online course is fulfilling its purpose, following the course outline, and meeting students' needs. Any reasonably competent administrator—even a technophobe or a neo-Luddite—should be able to make those determinations.

The original essay was published March 11, 2010, in *The Chronicle of Higher Education.*

> Even though you may no longer be close friends with members of your department, you now have an even greater responsibility toward them: You are essentially the firewall between them and vindictive students, angry parents, and crusading administrators.

WHAT NEW DEPARTMENT CHAIRS NEED TO KNOW

Perhaps the most difficult transition a person can make, professionally speaking, is from rank and file to management—from being one of the gang to supervising and evaluating it. That's especially true in higher education, where we place such value on collegiality, autonomy, and egalitarianism. As a new chair, you're probably painfully aware that most of your friends are now former colleagues whom you supervise. To complicate matters, they're actually still your colleagues. *And* you supervise them. Since you're the chair, they now view you differently, as do students and other administrators. They all expect certain things from you. And there's no way you can meet all of those expectations, especially since some of them conflict.

I don't mean to be overly negative. Chairing a department is a worthwhile way to spend part of your academic career. Two-year colleges need good department chairs in order to function well—or function at all. But if you don't mind, I'll leave the cheerleading (such as it is) for the end of this column. First you need to understand what you're up against. After observing department chairs for 25 years (some good, some not) and spending 10 years as a department head myself, here's what I've learned.

You Need New Friends

Of course, you don't have to stop being friendly with your faculty colleagues, and you certainly don't have to stop liking them. But you do have to accept that it's no longer appropriate for you to pal around with particular individuals or groups—going to lunch, socializing outside of work, spending inordinate amounts of time chatting. That's because those activities will very likely create animosity, distrust, and suspicion among faculty members with whom you do not share a close relationship. You will also open yourself up to charges of favoritism and bias as you complete evaluations, schedule courses, and make committee assignments. Seek out a new group of friends from among those at roughly your same level on the organizational chart: other department chairs, department heads in nonacademic areas, and program directors. Or socialize with people who are technically below (or above) you on that chart but whose jobs are unconnected to your own, such as counselors and librarians.

The good news, of course, is that even though you are leaving some old friends behind—and may never be as close to them again, even if you return to the faculty after a few years—you stand to make some new friends. You are also forming a support group of people whose work situations are similar to yours and perhaps making connections that will benefit you throughout your career. After all, one of those other chairs might well be dean one day.

Your Default Mode Should Be Pro-Faculty

Even though you may no longer be close friends with members of your department, you now have an even greater responsibility toward them: You are essentially the firewall between them and vindictive students, angry parents, and crusading administrators. When I first became chair, I thought my job was to keep faculty members, administrators, and students all happy. I quickly figured out that that was impossible. The chair's real job is to keep faculty members happy without annoying administrators and students too much.

Having just recently left the faculty ranks, your natural loyalties probably lie in that direction. But there's another reason for taking a pro-faculty stance: You're the only administrator who will. Sure, deans can be pro-faculty, to a point, but the nature of their jobs often requires them to take a wider view. I've always believed it's the chair's job to stand up for faculty members, and a chair who is unwilling to do so will not have much success.

That doesn't mean your department members will always be right (although I've found over the years that they usually are, especially in grade disputes). There may be times when you simply have to acknowledge that the faculty member is wrong and take steps to rectify a situation. But initially, at least, when everyone else on the campus is coming down on a faculty member, it's important for you to be on his or her side. That may be the single most important way to build trust in your department. Which segues neatly into my next point:

Trust Is the Key

A friend of mine who is a basketball coach says that, in his profession, there's a continuing debate over whether it's more important for players to respect the coach or to like him. I have to admit that when I first became a department chair, I wondered about the same thing. The answer, I soon learned, is that neither respect nor affection is the most important element in your relationship with faculty members. More important by far is that they trust you.

Trust, in this context, means several things. It means that faculty members believe they can talk to you about anything, that you'll keep those conversations to yourself, and that you won't hold what they say in private against them. A department chair who is a backbiter or a gossip, or who simply divulges sensitive information to other faculty members, is likely to have a very short, miserable, and unsuccessful tenure. (Or to be promoted. It's a toss-up.)

Trust also means that faculty members believe you will do what you say. When you agree to something or promise something or say that you will take care of something, they must be able to take you at your word. And the only way to earn that kind of trust is, over time, to keep your word consistently and live up to your commitments—even when doing so is inconvenient. Finally, as I mentioned already, trust means that faculty members know you have their backs. Absolutely nothing is more important to department morale than that.

It's a Desk Job

For me, one of the hardest things about becoming a department chair was giving up so much personal freedom. As a faculty member I had a set schedule—classes, office hours, committee meetings—but those things rarely consumed an entire 8-hour day. And other than that I could pretty much come and go as I pleased. Department chairs, however, are basically chained to their desks from 8 a.m. to 5 p.m., 5 days a week, 250 days a year, except to attend various and sundry meetings. (You know your job is tedious when you look forward to a committee meeting.)

As chair, you have a lot of paperwork: class schedules, workload reports, adjunct applications, faculty evaluations, crossword puzzles. But the truth is, whether you're actually doing anything or not, you simply need to be sitting at your desk so people can find you when they want to complain. And by people I mean anyone with a gripe, including but not limited to students, faculty members, counselors, custodians, bookstore managers, vending machine operators, department secretaries, public safety officers, other department heads, and upper-level administrators. Why? Because. . . .

You-Know-What Flows Downhill

If you make the rookie mistake of actually looking at the organizational chart, you may subscribe to the popular misconception that, although deans and vice presidents are clearly above you, faculty members are below you. In other words, you're in the middle—hence the term "middle management." That view is not entirely accurate. You are in the middle, but only in the sense of being between a proverbial rock and a hard place. Otherwise you are not really below deans and above faculty members, but rather below both of them. Students, too. Imagine those three groups as the sides of a triangular-shaped basin. You are the drain.

OK, I'm exaggerating, but the fact remains that administrators will blame you for what faculty members do, faculty members will blame you for what administrators do, and students will blame you for everything. The trick is to figure out which complaints are valid and which ones you can actually do something about. Then deal with those, and basically ignore the rest. With a little wisdom, a little hard work, and a lot of luck, you'll solve enough real problems that the petty or imaginary ones will fade into the background.

No doubt you're thinking that the picture I've presented of chairing a department is pretty bleak, and that maybe you've made a mistake accepting the job. Maybe you did, but not necessarily. As I said at the outset, being a department chair can be a tremendously rewarding experience. In fact, when it comes to making a difference in people's lives every day, you really can't beat it. Because, in the end, that's what a department chair really is: someone who makes it possible for other people to accomplish their goals—for teachers to teach, students to study, administrators to, uh, administer. Being a department head is not easy, and it's not always fun, but somebody needs to do it. And right at this moment, maybe it's good that it's you.

The original essay was published October 20, 2009, in *The Chronicle of Higher Education.*

Appendix A

Online Resources

American Association of Community Colleges (www.aacc.nche.edu)
- A wealth of data and information about two-year colleges
- Daily news and job postings in *Community College Times* online (www.communitycollegetimes.com/)
- Community College Press online bookstore (www.aacc.nche.edu/bookstore)

Chronicle.com
- Job list
- Job market discussion forum (chronicle.com/forums/)

ERIC Clearinghouse for Community Colleges (www.eric.ed.gov)
- Database of journal articles and documents relating to community colleges

Inside Higher Ed (www.insidehighered.com)
- Daily news updates
- Job search

League for Innovation in the Community College (www.league.org)
- Information on its member colleges
- Jobnet

Modern Language Association (www.mla.org)
- Job information lists
- Committee on Community Colleges resources (see Appendix B)
- Job counseling opportunities at the MLA annual meeting

National Council of Teachers of English (www.ncte.org)
- The Two-Year College English Association (www.ncte.org/groups/tyca)
- *Teaching English in the Two-Year College*
- Conference on College Composition and Communication (4C's) (www.ncte.org/cccc/)—an annual conference that includes job interviews

Appendix B

A Community College Teaching Career
MLA Committee on Community Colleges, 2006

Publisher's Note. The Modern Language Association's (MLA's) Committee on Community Colleges is charged with working, through June 2015, on a range of issues that affect modern language teachers in 2-year colleges, including conditions of employment, staffing, curriculum, articulation with secondary schools and 4-year institutions, and the preparation and recruitment of faculty members. This appendix contains an excerpt, in near entirety, from the committee's report, A Community College Teaching Career. *Although targeted to language instructors, you will find that the advice is applicable to anyone interested in a community college career, which makes the report a very useful complement to this volume. The report can also be downloaded from the MLA website (http://www.mla.org/ccc), along with two other very useful documents:* Considering Community Colleges: Advice to Graduate Students and Job Seekers *and* Selected Annotated Bibliography on Community College Teaching, 1993–2003.

1. WHY CONSIDER A CAREER IN THE COMMUNITY COLLEGE?

When you open up your job search to the community college, a tremendous range of opportunities that satisfies practical as well as career goals becomes available. Our brief essay provides introductory material that will help you explore this option as we cover characteristics of two-year colleges and their students, professional opportunities and challenges for faculty members, the peculiarities of the two-year-college job search, adjunct teaching as a career path, and resources for the job search. Approximately 22% of all full-time faculty members teach in two-year colleges; they do so for the opportunity to make an impact in the lives of their students and in their communities.

General Characteristics

The first public community college, Joliet Junior College, opened in 1901, and since then community colleges have placed publicly funded higher education, open to all, close to home. According to the American Association of Community Colleges Web site, as of January 2006 there were 986 public two-year colleges in the United States and 29 tribal colleges; including independent two-year colleges and branch campuses, there were 1,600 community colleges. These institutions may be called junior colleges, tribal colleges, technical colleges, two-year colleges, or community colleges. (The terms "two-year college" and "community college" will be used interchangeably throughout this document to refer to all two-year colleges, unless otherwise noted.) Also known as "the people's colleges," community colleges are regionally accredited and award the associate degree as their highest credential (Pierce 3). Although all two-year colleges are "centers of educational opportunity," they also vary: "Each community college is a distinct educational institution, loosely linked to other community colleges by the shared goals of access and service. Open admissions and the tradition of charging low tuition are among the practices they have in common" (Amer. Assn. of Community Colls.).

Most community colleges (58%) are characterized as "small," enrolling under 4,500 students, while only8% are "extra large," with enrollments of 15,000 students or higher (*Engaging* 23). They are equally likely to be located in rural (37%) and urban (39%) areas, with the remaining 24% in suburban areas (*Engaging*23). These colleges offer lower-division general education and major preparation courses leading to an associate degree and/or transfer to a four-year college or university (the transfer education function). They also provide education and training in selected occupational fields leading to job entry, advancement, retraining, and certification and to associate degrees (the career-oriented function). Community colleges also provide transitional education programs and courses for students needing preparation to succeed in college-level work (the basic skills and adult education function). Both English courses and foreign language courses fulfill requirements for students on each of these three paths.

In terms of the sheer number of students they reach, two-year colleges have an enormous impact on American higher education. The California Community College System alone is composed of 109 colleges, serves more than 2.5 million students, and is the largest system of public higher education in the world, according to the system's Chancellor's Office Web page. A recent United States Department of Education analysis conducted by Clifford Adelman shows that roughly two-fifths of traditional-age students (18-24) began their college education at the community college; three-fifths of students over the age of 24 entered college at the community college. As of 2006, the American Association of Community Colleges reported that about 11.6 million students were enrolled in two-year colleges, 6.6 million in credit-bearing courses; these colleges award over 486,000 associate degrees and 235,000 certificates annually. Community college enrollment is expected to grow and the colleges to confer more associate degrees as the overall US population increases.

Who attends a two-year college? The most recent data from the American Association of Community Colleges indicate that the average age of the community college student is 29 and about 47% receive financial aid. Currently, more women than men enroll in US colleges, and this is even more true of two-year colleges, where 59% of the enrollees are female and 41% male. Although most community college students are in the middle socioeconomically and educationally (Leinbach), Adelman's review of United States Department of Education data finds that students from the lowest quintile socioeconomic status are increasingly more likely to begin postsecondary education at a community college. Thirty years ago, Adelman notes, 44% of these students started their coursework at community colleges; today 55% do. One reason is that community colleges are more affordable: the average cost of tuition and fees at a public two-year college in 2005-06 was $2,191, as opposed to $5,491 for in-state tuition and fees at a public four-year college and $21,235 at a private four-year college (Baum and Payea). Two groups of minority students are more likely to begin college at the two-year level, Hispanics (55% of whom attend community colleges)and Native Americans (57% of whom do), whereas African Americans (47%) and Asians and Pacific Islanders (47%) are slightly less likely to do so, according to the American Association of Community Colleges.

Community College Teaching: A Rewarding and Challenging Profession

Most two-year-college faculty members find their work deeply satisfying. A recent national survey of community college faculty members found that 73% report experiencing "joy" in their work and 71% believe their work is meaningful ("Views" B10). Teaching is a mission, not just a job, because community college faculty members change lives every day. But this work is not for everyone, as Anne Breznau has argued in an *ADE Bulletin* essay: "It is for the committed teacher who wants to help all kinds of people make better lives for themselves. It is also for the teacher-citizen who is ready to become involved in creating a better institution within the culture of a local community he or she is willing to call home."

As Breznau's phrase "all kinds of people" suggests, students in the typical community college class have a wide range of ages and life experiences and varying degrees of academic preparation. Students' ages may run from 16 to 80. Some are still in high school, some are ready to transfer to a university, and some hold advanced degrees. While this diversity is exciting, it also makes community college teaching more challenging. Instructors must be flexible and creative to meet these students' needs. A one-size-fits-all pedagogy simply does not work at a community college. As an English instructor chairing a hiring committee commented in an interview, two-year colleges need experienced teachers "who [can] go into the classroom with a bunch of twenty-five people with twenty-five different interests all going in different directions and get them focused and keep them focused" (qtd. in Twombly 432).

In addition to being "diverse" in the broadest sense, community college students are three to four times more likely than their four-year counterparts to need remediation, to delay their entry to college after graduating from high school, to enroll part-time, to be single parents, to have children, to work more than thirty hours a week, to be financially independent, and to be the first in their families to attend college—all factors that make them "high risk" (*Engaging* 5). In fact, almost half of all new community college students are "underprepared" as measured by institutional placement assessments (*Engaging* 6). At the same time, however, two-year-college students tend to be goal oriented and highly motivated. Research shows that teaching them can be tremendously satisfying because they are more likely to be "engaged" in their education in terms of spending more time studying and writing papers, working harder to meet instructors' expectations, attending class regularly, and coming to class prepared (*Engaging* 5).

Another reward—and challenge—is that faculty members at community colleges are expected to be proficient in the use of instructional technologies, including presentation software like PowerPoint, teaching in classrooms equipped with the latest technology ("smart" classrooms), developing supplemental Web sites for their classes, teaching online or through other distance learning media like cable TV, developing independent learning sections of foreign language courses, and so on. While new technologies are transforming how higher education delivers courses, their uses are particularly important at community colleges given their mission of making education accessible and accommodating students' different learning styles.

A Unique Opportunity: Relations with K–12 Systems and Four-Year Transfer Partners

As part of their "community" role, community colleges typically develop close relationships not only with other colleges in their districts but also with local K–12 systems and nearby universities. Usually, a community college has an identified set of "feeder districts" whose students attend that college because of its proximity. In turn, the community college sends the majority of its transfer students to a core group of four-year institutions. It is thus in the best interests of the community college student for the institution to have close professional ties to these transfer partners. Alternately, of course, some two-year colleges are regional campuses within a university. Transfer from the two-year college is articulated through program design and agreements with the partner college.

Two-year-college faculty members are often asked to do outreach to the local K–12 systems both to articulate coursework and to publicize programs to recruit new students. Many community colleges sponsor visitation days for high school students and even for elementary school students, especially those in less advantaged districts, to encourage student goal setting to include attendance at the community college. Faculty members open their classes for visitations, which can build enrollment while serving the community.

Instructors may also be involved in meetings with the faculty of their disciplines at nearby four-year institutions to assist articulation and transfer efforts for community college students. Some colleges have assigned outreach administrators to facilitate such meetings. In other cases, they are faculty generated. Such meetings can facilitate networking and participation in area grant proposals, student exchanges, and curriculum development. Placed in "the middle," the community college program needs close alignment with its transfer partners at each end if students are to be well served. These considerations are unique to the community college and can foster very satisfying professional activities.

Your Role as [an] Instructor

Several aspects of community college teaching are clearly distinct from those of the four-year college.

- **Teaching load.** Because teaching is the central role of a community college instructor, the teaching load at a two-year college is generally heavier than at a four-year institution. Fifteen units a semester is common, which translates into about four foreign language courses or five English courses a semester. Class sizes may also be larger than average. According to the 2004 National Study of Postsecondary Faculty, faculty members at public community colleges spend an average of 18.1 hours a week teaching and have 431 contact hours (the number of hours teaching multiplied by the total number of students enrolled in courses) a week, as opposed to an average of only 8.1 hours teaching and 287 contact hours a week for faculty members at public doctoral institutions (Cataldi, Bradburn, and Fahimi 31).
- **Absence of teaching assistants** in the grading of papers and the offering of sections of introductory classes. Student assistants may be available for tutoring and small-group work, but practices vary.

- **Requirements for reappointment, promotion, and tenure.** Evidence of teaching excellence, not research, is the means by which most community colleges award tenure and promote faculty members, at institutions where tenure and promotion are available. Research is viewed as an add-on after success in teaching except for two-year colleges that are incorporated into four-year university systems, which usually do require research and publication. Faculty members at public community colleges report spending 79.8% of their time teaching but only 3.5% on research, compared with public doctoral university faculty members, who report spending 50.8% of their time teaching and 28.2% on research (Cataldi, Bradburn, and Fahimi 29).

- **Salaries.** The American Association of University Professors (AAUP) publishes annual surveys of faculty salaries. In many areas of the country salaries at two-year colleges are competitive with (and sometimes exceed) those of neighboring four-year colleges. The 2005-06 AAUP survey shows that the average salary for full-time faculty members at two-year public colleges with ranks is $52,719 compared to $56,902 at public four-year colleges ("Devaluing" 37), with salaries varying regionally from a low average of $45,336 in East South Central states to a high average of $59,061 in the Middle Atlantic states ("Devaluing" 39). The faculties of many public community colleges are unionized, and salary advancement is structured, based on years of service and on rank at some colleges. This may mean more regular increases than at four-year institutions, where a number of factors influence these adjustments and advancements may not be automatic.

- **Rank.** Some institutions call all faculty members "Instructors." At other colleges, academic rank (Instructor, Assistant Professor, Associate Professor, and Professor) is determined by such factors as degree, promotion, and years of service.

- **Office hours.** The number is often set by union contract. Five to ten hours a week are not unusual.

- **Opportunities for administrative roles.** Foreign languages and English are often set in a division rather than in, for example, a College of Arts and Sciences, which is more common at the four-year institution. Two-year colleges often fill positions of division chairs or deans internally, allowing faculty members who aspire to administrative roles the opportunity to serve in a leadership role while retaining the right to return to a tenured teaching position if they choose.

- **Teaching assignments.** Foreign language instructors can expect to spend the bulk of their time teaching the first four semesters of language study. In heavily enrolled languages, there will also likely be separate courses for conversation, culture, composition, introduction to literature, and language for business purposes. Film, women's studies, and comparative literature courses are possible as well. For English instructors, courses range from basic reading and writing and ESL courses to university-parallel composition and literature courses, honors courses, creative writing, technical and professional writing, and genre and survey courses in literature. As with the foreign languages, English faculty members may have the opportunity to teach film, cultural studies, humanities, journalism, and so on, depending on their background and training. Usually, however, new two-year English faculty members teach composition.

2. THE HIRING PROCESS

The hiring process for any individual community college position may be different from that of a four-year institution and may vary widely from that of a different community college. Candidates who apply for a position at a two-year college should be aware of these differences from the out-set and adjust their expectations accordingly. The following paragraphs sketch out some of these differences and the reasons behind them. Please note, though, that hiring practices at two-year colleges are as diverse as the colleges themselves. Always ask the college for clarification if the process is not clear.

The Position Itself

Colleges usually have a campus-wide mechanism for deciding which positions will be opened in a given year. The proposal for a new position begins with the department, but the process of obtaining a new full-time line is competitive, based on the projected college budget for the next year and enrollment and program demands as measured by statistical data. New positions may not be announced until late in the fall semester or early in the spring semester. It is also common to advertise in the summer for temporary full-time positions replacing faculty members on leave or unexpected retirees.

The Processes

These are often controlled by the college governing board policy, union agreements, and strict state guidelines for public community colleges. The human resources department often directs the process and may require a standard format for the interviews and similar interaction of committee members with all candidates. Human resources will often be the first point of contact for com-munity college applicants. Typically, candidates should expect less social interaction with those making hiring decisions at a public community college than at four-year colleges or universities, especially private ones. The hiring process may not include lunch or dinner with department faculty members, a campus tour, or even a coffee break. Job candidates should not be put off by these practices; while candidates may interpret community college hiring practices as impersonal or unfriendly, community colleges are simply striving to treat all candidates equally.

The Budget for the Interview Process

Historically, budgets for hiring are very limited at two-year colleges. In part, this may be due to the fact that community colleges, even when they advertise nationally, tend to attract enough quali-fied candidates regionally, thus avoiding the expenses of a true national search (Twombly 438-41; Breznau). Advertising for a position may take place in the *Chronicle of Higher Education*, in local newspapers, and in any statewide registries of positions. Rarely do community colleges send a committee to the annual MLA convention. Many colleges pay no travel expenses for on-campus interviews, while some will award a stipend, if it is requested, especially to low-income or under-represented group candidates. The candidate should learn what expenses, if any, will be paid be-fore agreeing to the interview.

3. SECRETS OF THE INTERVIEW

How to Get an Interview

Although the exact sequence of steps in the hiring process differs from college to college, the patterns we describe are common practice. The initial interview committee usually is selected to represent the whole college, not just the discipline, with about 5–12 members including faculty members in the discipline and related fields, employees from other offices of the college, a student, an administrator, and so forth. This committee will screen the applications. If your field is English or Spanish there may be three hundred applications for the fifteen or fewer interviews that will occur. Some colleges use phone interviews as an initial screening device as well. (For specific tips on how to handle phone interviews, see Breznau.) If you are selected for an interview, you will be contacted by a department administrator or the human relations department to arrange an interview time. To enhance your chances of being selected, consider these suggestions:

- Respond exactly to the questions on the application and those of any assigned essay. Be sure to complete all required forms and submit all required letters and transcripts, if any, on time. Consider developing two versions of your curriculum vitae, one for a community college job search and one for four-year colleges. On the community college CV, emphasize teaching experience and interests, community involvement and volunteer work, and experience on college or university committees. Also, consider creating a job match sheet that lists in one column every qualification identified in the announcement and shows in a second column how you meet or exceed the minimum qualifications of each of these. This makes it very clear to the committee why you should be interviewed. You do not want to make a harried committee member search hard to discover how you meet these qualifications.

  Many states have minimum qualifications by discipline that guide the hiring of community college instructors. The MA in your field is the typical minimum requirement, although many candidates possess a PhD. Meeting the minimum qualifications does not, of course, guarantee an interview. If you do not meet the posted job requirements, do not apply. It is common for screening committees to eliminate half of all applicants because they do not meet requirements or do not follow directions, a waste of time and energy for everyone involved (Breznau; Kort).

- Compose your cover letter carefully. This 1-2-page letter should bring the CV to life, not merely restate information on the CV. The letter should highlight your qualifications that meet the requirements of the prospective job, including graduate work that is relevant to teaching, but it may be desirable to downplay your research interests if they are not relevant to the position. And keep your audience in mind: the committee will be looking for evidence of your ability to communicate effectively with readers of all kinds. The letter should be clearly written and free from theoretical or technical jargon.

- If the job notice does not preclude it, include materials in your application that demonstrate evidence of your teaching ability, such as teaching evaluations. Ask those who write your letters of reference to observe your classes and to include comments about your teaching in their letters.

Planning for the Interview

- Research the college, its campus, and its community beforehand. The college Web site and catalog should provide good basic information. Read the mission statement of the college. Try to read also (online or at the college library) a copy of the college's last accreditation self-study or the college master plan. These documents often include details about the student population and the population in the area served by the community college and frequently current issues and current directions of your proposed department as well.
- Become familiar with the history of the community college movement, and spend time reflecting on your pedagogical practices. Community colleges seek candidates who display an unconditional commitment to and regard for students from diverse backgrounds who need faculty members to guide them through the transition from work or high school to college-level study. The idea of weeding students out or tossing them into the pool and exhorting them to "sink or swim" runs counter to the ethos of community college teaching.
- Arrive early and talk with students on the campus. Pay attention to student demographics but recognize that community colleges have different populations for day and evening or weekend classes. Reference what you have learned about the students during your interview.
- Plan out how to present yourself to your best advantage in your introductory and concluding comments. What do you want the committee to remember about you? What distinguishes you from the other candidates?
- Consider how you will respond to common interview questions asked by screening committees.

Common Interview Questions

- Why are you interested in teaching at a community college? What is your understanding of the mission of a community college?
- What are the greatest challenges for higher education in the next ten years? for community colleges and their missions?
- What service contributions can you make to this college?
- What contributions can you make to your profession through your work at this college?
- Describe your experiences with developmental education or with meeting the needs of students with disabilities. Describe your experiences incorporating technology into your teaching.
- Explain specifically how you incorporate the concept of diversity into your classes.
- What are your experiences with distance learning?
- What have you done in your courses to maximize students' success in learning?
- How do you identify students' needs and how do you meet them in and out of class? Give specific examples.
- What do you know about our college or student population?
- What experiences have you had with defining student learning outcomes and assessing them?

- What's your greatest teaching success? Why? What's your greatest teaching failure? How did you handle it? What have you learned from it?
- How did you prepare for this interview today?

(*Note.* See the original for sample questions specific to instructors applying for foreign language and English positions.)

Other General Points

- Be prepared to demonstrate your teaching skills as part of the initial screening interview. Candidates are often asked to teach a short lesson, sometimes on an assigned topic. Ask about time limits, audience, and other parameters, if possible, before you come to campus. If you get to choose your topic, remember that demonstrations of your ability to teach a well-defined, concrete concept work best, especially when they address common problems in the discipline. Above all, committees are interested in *your* presentation skills. One administrator on an interviewing committee explains how candidates are evaluated: "Do they stand up there and just give a straight lecture? Do they just talk to us? Their eye contact is absent. Do they just kind of meander up there? . . . Do they engage the audience? Do they use interactive things? . . . What types of learning activities do they include?" (qtd. in Twombly 436).
- Have a few suitable questions in mind to ask about the position or your department or the college, if given the chance. Committees are not impressed by candidates who have no questions or who only want to know about salary and benefits or opportunities for teaching more advanced courses or for obtaining released time for research. Instead, ask about the administrative structure of the college (if that has not already been made clear), opportunities for faculty development, the reappointment, promotion and tenure procedure, challenges facing the college, and opportunities to serve on committees or to become involved with student groups or the community. Let the committee know that you will engage with the institution if hired.
- Be aware of the time limits of the interview and be sure your answers are delivered in a succinct, energetic manner. The committee will be observing you closely during the interview to determine how you will engage with students.
- What not to do? This is not the place for an exhaustive study of poor interviewing technique, which would be similar at any rate in a four-year or two-year interview. Do realize that the committee is seeking an instructor committed to the specific mission of that community college with a focus on teaching. Committee members want to assure themselves that you are really interested in a career at their college, not just interviewing there as a second choice because there is no position down the road at the university. Be clear in your mind about your commitment to the position and be sure that this commitment is communicated to the committee.

What Else to Expect at the First Interview

Some colleges have only one interview while others have a committee interview followed by an administrative interview for finalists. Your initial interview will probably last one to two hours. Interview questions are often reviewed in advance by human resources personnel and administrators before being assigned by the screening committee chair to individual committee members to ask. All candidates will be asked the same questions, usually in the same order, though follow-up questions may differ depending on your answers. The committee's need to ensure uniformity and fairness can give the interview a stilted feel, but do not take this personally or be put off by it. You may be offered a tour of the campus on the day of the interview, but this is not a given. Community college instructors teach several hours every day, so interviews and tours are wedged into this schedule. Wise committee members realize that they are "selling" the campus to the candidates as much as the reverse, but the time-limited format of the community college interview does not necessarily support this effort.

The Finalist Interview(s)

After the initial interviews are concluded, the committee may have the authority to rank candidates or maybe able only to make recommendations and present perhaps three to five names to the administration. Some colleges simply offer the position to the top-ranked candidate at this point. Other colleges invite the top candidates to a second interview with a dean or vice president. If you are invited to this second interview and are interested in the position, do accept the invitation! Do not hesitate to mention financial limitations and ask for support if this is a factor for you. Often, accommodation can be arranged through teleconferencing or a telephone interview if finalists do not live within commuting distance of the college.

If you are chosen for the position, some colleges arrange for you to meet with the college president for final approval and negotiation of placement on the salary schedule, based on past teaching experience. At some public community colleges, you are only "hired" officially after the governing board meets (usually biweekly or monthly) and approves your hiring.

4. THE ADJUNCT POSITION AT THE COMMUNITY COLLEGE

The discussion above has been directed to those seeking a full-time, tenure-track position at a community college. What about the part-time or adjunct position—either as a route to obtaining a full-time position or simply as an alternative? Throughout their history, community colleges have hired part-time instructors for the occupational expertise they bring to the classroom. In more recent decades, as public funding has tightened, community colleges have begun to rely more on adjunct faculty members across the curriculum as a way to keep salary costs down. Adjunct instructors are usually limited to teaching up to 60% of the annual load of a contract faculty member at the institution. And although the minimum qualifications for adjunct and full-time positions are often identical, the pay per course is often only a fraction of what the full-time faculty member receives. The AAUP analyzed United States Department of Education data for2003 and found that the salary per course at public two-year colleges ranged from a low of $1,397 at the25th percentile to a high of $3,000 at the 90th percentile; in hourly wages, the median pay for an adjunct at a two-year college was only $11.19 ("Devaluing" 33). This limited pay from any single institution leads many adjuncts to teach part-time at two or three colleges to earn a living wage, yielding the phenomenon of the "free-way flyer."

Some institutions (the colleges of the University of Cincinnati are one such example) have a new layer of adjunct faculty, field service representatives, who are full-time, untenured faculty members, with indefinite reappointment possibilities. They receive the same minimum pay and benefits as tenure-track faculty members and have obligations to faculty development and service. This example is but one indication of greatly varying options for adjunct faculty members at two-year colleges.

Is there any good reason to accept this employment while searching for a job if a permanent position is your goal? It is difficult to suggest to graduate students that they consider being underpaid in such a position with few reemployment rights. But here are several reasons to consider such a position:

- Teaching at a community college for a semester or two is the best way to determine if this kind of work suits you.
- Having teaching experience at the community college will often make a difference between getting or not getting an interview when a full-time position opens up and may be important for being offered the position as well. Two-year colleges often favor the candidate with teaching experience at a community college over the candidate with a higher degree and university teaching experience. The interview questions themselves will resonate differently with each candidate. The answers of candidates who have already taught at the community college will tend to ring more true, especially as to their commitment to teaching at this level.
- Successful adjunct instructors may have a better chance to obtain a full-time position at the institution where they have been teaching, if that experience has been successful. Although many community college administrators view good part-time faculty members as a pool of potential tenure-track hires (Twombly 441), adjunct experience does not guarantee that you will be interviewed for a tenure-track position, which often leads to hurt feelings among the part-time staff.
- If your search is limited to one geographic area because of family commitments or continuing work with your graduate institution as you complete your doctorate, it may make sense to interview for a part-time position at a neighboring college and begin being known by the faculty in the institutions of your area. Again, since two-year colleges tend to hire from within a region, you may have an advantage over candidates who are not familiar with the community and its students.
- If you accept an adjunct position, take advantage of opportunities to work with your colleagues and get to know the field (as time permits). Attending faculty meetings and serving on committees allows you to stay informed about your field and about college life, even though this service is usually optional for adjunct faculty members. Use student evaluations and supervisor or peer evaluations to your advantage; when your evaluations are

good, ask those who observed your class to serve as references or write you a letter of recommendation.

Individuals will need to decide for themselves if adjunct teaching is a legitimate step on a career path in two-year college teaching.

WORKS CITED

Adelman, Clifford. "Executive Summary: Moving into Town—and Moving On: The Community College in the Lives of Traditional-Age Students." US Dept. of Educ. Office of Vocational and Adult Education. Feb.2005. 19 Oct. 2006 (http://www.ed.gov/print/rschstat/research/pubs/comcollege/index.html)

American Association of Community Colleges. 2006. 15 June 2006 (http://w ww.aacc.nche.edu/) Path: About Community Colleges; Fast Facts.

Baum, Sandy, and Kathleen Payea. "Trends in College Pricing 2005." *College Board*. Trends in Higher Education Series. 2005. 19 May 2006 (http://www.collegeboard.com/trends)

Breznau, Anne. "Operationalized Democracy: Teaching English at the Community College." *ADE Bulletin* Fall 1998: 21–23. 1998. 20 Feb. 2006 (http://www.mla.org/ade/bulletin/n120/120021.htm)

Cataldi, Emily F., Ellen M. Bradburn, and Mansour Fahimi. *2004 National Study of Postsecondary Faculty(NSOPF: 04): Background Characteristics, Work Activities, and Compensation of Instructional Faculty and Staff: Fall 2003*. US Dept. of Educ. Natl. Center for Educ. Statistics. Dec. 2005. 19 May 2006 (http://nces.ed.gov/pubsearch)

California Community Colleges. Chancellor's Office. 2005. 15 June 2006 (http://www.cccco.edu/) "The Devaluing of Higher Education: The Annual Report on the Economic Status of the Profession 20052006." *Academe* Mar.–Apr. 2006: 24–105.

Engaging Students, Challenging the Odds. CCSSE: Community College Survey of Student Engagement.2005 Findings. Community College Leadership Program, Austin: 2005.

Kort, Melissa Sue. "PhD at the JC? Preparing Teachers for Two-Year Colleges." *ADE Bulletin* 122 (1999): 65–67. 20 Feb. 2006 (http://www.mla.org/ade/bulletin/n122/122065.htm)

Leinbach, Timothy. "Studying Students Moving into Higher Education . . . to a Community College?!" *Teachers College Record* 19 Aug. 2005. 19 Cct. 2005 (http://www.tcrecord.org/PrintContent. asp?ContentID=12125)

Pierce, David. "What You Need to Know about Two-Year Colleges." *Peterson's Two-Year Colleges 2006*. Lawrenceville: Thomson Peterson's, 2006. 3–5.

Twombly, Susan B. "Values, Policies, and Practices Affecting the Hiring Process for Full-Time Arts and Sciences Faculty in Community Colleges." *Journal of Higher Education* 76 (2005): 423–447.

"Views and Characteristics of Community College Professors." *Chronicle of Higher Education* 28 Nov. 2005: B10.

Index

Aa

academic freedom, 16, 112, 113
accreditation, 38–43
Adams, Henry, 102
Adelman, Clifford, 11
American Association of Community
      Colleges (AACC), 13–14
application for faculty position at community
      college, 29–34
   collegiality and, 46, 47, 48–49
   cover letter in, 30–31, 33–34, 45–46, 57
   CV and, 30. *see also* CV
   handling of, after submission, 32–33
   known adjuncts versus outside applicants
      and, 50–52, 79–80
   making it stand out, 32–34
   minimum qualifications and, 44–45, 47
   references included with, 31, 33
   résumé and. *see* résumé
   teaching experience and, 45–46, 51
   understanding of community college
      mission and, 46, 47–48, 51,
      61–62
   willingness to work beyond classroom
      and, 46, 47, 48
Atlantic Monthly, 108

Bb

Benson, Melanie, 21, 23
Branded, 102

Cc

cattle call, 70–72, 74
The Chronicle of Higher Education
   blog of, 19
   essays in, 21, 58, 73, 85, 102, 129
   faculty positions advertised in, 3, 43
class blog, 97
community college(s)
   academic department structure at, 36.
      see also department chair
   accreditation and, 38–43
   administration in. *see* community college
      administration
   admission policies of, 10, 47–48, 61
   budgets and, 3–4, 60, 81, 95, 100, 125
   committee work at, 91–92, 106
   criticism of, 10–14
   faculty adviser at, 57, 92
   honors programs at, 10
   human resource (HR) departments at,
      29, 32
   interviewing at. *see* interview at
      community college
   mission of, 46, 47–48, 51, 61–62, 95
   professors in. *see* professor(s) in
      community colleges
   public perceptions of, 15
   research in, 3, 25, 26, 47, 60, 69, 94, 95
   search committees at. *see* search
      committee
   sizes of, 11
   students in. *see* students in community
      colleges
   teaching load in, 3, 17, 23, 26, 66, 69,
      94, 117
   textbook selection at, 16

travel funding available in, 3–4, 60, 95, 125

tuition at, 10, 100

work environment at, 16

community college administration

complaints from students about faculty and, 129–131

department chair and, 120–122, 142–145

fictional character Albus Dumbledore as model for, 135–137

"high school mentality" of, 15–17

interference in search process by, 80–81

pros and cons of getting into, 117–119

salaries in, 117

special requests from students and, 126–128

trust and, 123–125, 143–144

working hours of, 118, 121, 144

conferences, professional, 4, 6, 17, 95, 125

Connors, Chuck, 102

continuing contract, 6. *see also* tenure

cover letter with job application, 30–31, 33–34, 45–46, 57

curriculum committee, 60, 91

CV

attached to job application, 30, 31

résumé versus, 31, 33

Dd

department chair, 120–122

new, what he or she needs to know, 142–145

department secretary, 105, 107

developmental courses, 10, 47, 56, 68

Digest of Education Statistics (2008), 13

distance learning, 138–141

doctorate(s)

cost of obtaining, 21–23

professors in community colleges having, 7, 18–19

teaching quality and, 7, 18–20, 37

Dumbledore, Albus, 135–137

Ff

faculty adviser, 57, 92

Fish, Stanley, 117

Frost, Robert, 108

Gg

The Grapes of Wrath, 50

Hh

Harry Potter and the Half-Blood Prince, 135

"high school mentality," 15–17

Ii

Internet chat room, 97

interview at community college, 58–78

appearance and, 68

appointment for, 58, 67–68

letter confirming, 58–59

cattle call and, 70–72, 74

failure to get job from, 79–81

how to stand out in, 67–69

performance at, 68–69

punctuality and, 67–68

questions asked by candidate during, 60, 69

questions asked by search committee during, 59, 68–69

talking too much during, 65

teaching demonstration during, 59–60, 69, 76–78

what not to do during, 64–66

Jj

job security, 6. *see also* tenure

Kk

Kierkegaard, Soren, 135

Kissinger, Henry, 48

Mm

Madonna, 48
M*A*S*H, 96, 98
mentoring, 92–93, 105–106
Munger, Michael C., 133

Oo

101 Things to Do with Ramen Noodles, 22
Onear, Peter, 12–14
organizational skills, 106–107

Pp

Pimp My Ride, 96
professor(s) in community colleges
    applying for job as. *see* application
        for faculty position at
        community college
    being low-maintenance and, 107
    collegiality and, 46, 47, 48–49, 107
    complaints from students about, 129–
        131
    conferences attended by, 4, 6, 17, 95,
        125
    credentials and, 38–43
    customer service and, 99–101
    employment benefits of, 4, 7, 23
    evaluation of, 85–90
    by peer or supervisor, 86
    self-, 85–86
    by students, 85, 86–87, 88–90
    having doctorates, 7, 18–19, 37
    humility and, 105–106
    institution funded travel by, 3–4, 60, 95,
        125
    mentoring and, 92–93, 105–106
    new
        to faculty, characteristics for success
            of, 105–107
        tips for, 102–104
    organizational skills and, 106–107
    position as stepping-stone to position in
        4-year institution and, 24–26
    prestige and, 4–5, 23
    professional development and, 94–95

professionalism of, 89, 101
    promotion and, 85, 91
    publishing by, 3, 6, 26, 85, 94–95
    quality of life enjoyed by, 7
    research by, 3, 25, 26, 47, 60, 69, 94,
        95
    salaries of, 4, 7, 23, 24, 70–71

    with second part-time job at another
        institution, 108–110
    service by, 91–93
        to community, 91, 93
        to institution, 91–93
    similarities of, to cats, 132–134
    teaching load of, 3, 17, 23, 26, 66, 69,
        117
    tenure and, 6, 24, 49, 52, 81, 85, 91,
        111–114
    trust of administrators and, 123–125,
        143–144
    trying to "break in" as, 55–57
    willingness to work beyond classroom
        and, 46, 47, 48, 91–92, 106
professors in 4-year institutions
    evaluation of, 85
    prestige and, 23
    publishing by, 6, 8, 85
    research by, 25, 26
    salaries of, 8, 23
    tenure and, 6, 112, 113
Proust, Marcel, 135

Rr

The Rare Breed, 21
RateMyProfessor.com, 96, 102
remedial or developmental courses, 10, 47,
    56, 68
research
    at community colleges, 3, 25, 26, 47,
        60, 69, 94, 95
    at 4-year institutions, 25, 26
résumé
    attached to job application, 31
    CV versus, 31, 33
    information to include in, 31, 57
Rowling, J. K., 135–137

Ss

search committee
    biases and, 74–75, 80
    characteristics sought by, 44–49, 52
    decisions by, 7, 24, 25, 32–33, 52,
        74–75, 79–81
    formation of, 57
    infighting on, 80
    making yourself attractive to, 29, 30
    patronizing and, 66
    personal agendas and, 80
    questions asked by during interview, 59,
        68–69
    questions candidate asks during
        interview, 60, 69
    service on, 70–72
    what should not be done by, 73–75
SmartBoard, 63, 97
Smith, Betsy, 50–51
Socrates, 9, 11
Stewart, Jimmy, 21
students in community colleges
    ages of, 11, 13–14
    complaints from, about faculty, 129–131
    as customers, 99–101
    diversity among, 9, 11, 47, 59
    evaluation of professors by, 85, 86–87,
        88–90
    learning styles of, 62
    quality of, 4, 10, 47–48, 59
    reasons for choosing to be, 10–11,
        13, 14
    remedial or developmental courses
        taken by, 10, 47, 56, 68
    special requests from, 126–128
Sun Tzu, 9

Tt

teaching
    as adjunct, 50–52, 56, 79–80, 92–93
    appearing confident and, 102–103
    of community college students, skills for,
        61–62

consistency in, 103
credentials and, 38–43
demonstration of, 59–60, 69, 76–78
doctorates and, 7, 18–20, 37
experience in, 45–46, 47, 51, 59, 69,
    71–72
description of, in cover letter, 30–31,
    33–34, 45–46, 57
learning outcomes and, 90
in multiple disciplines, 35–37
by new teacher, tips for, 102–104
online courses and, 138–141
part time, 55, 56–57, 79–80, 92–93,
    108–110
"performance aspect" of, 138
record of success in, 6, 26, 45–46, 47,
    51
rewards of, 5, 7–8
as second job, 108–110
technology used in, 62–63, 78, 86,
    96–98
teaching demonstration, 59–60, 69, 76–78
tenure
    academic freedom and, 112, 113
    in community colleges, 6, 24, 49, 52,
        81, 85, 91, 111–114
    in 4-year institutions, 6, 112, 113
    revocation of, 112
Toth, Emily, 85
Trading Spaces, 96

Ww

Wheelan, Belle, 41–42, 43
whiteboard technology, 63, 97

Zz

Zimbleman, Dana M., 58

About the Author

During his 20-year career in higher education—nearly all of it spent at 2-year colleges, Rob Jenkins has worked for six different institutions as a part-time faculty member, a department chair, an academic dean, and a program director. He is currently an associate professor of English and director of the Writers Institute at Georgia Perimeter College. He holds a master's degree in writing from the University of Tennessee and has completed additional graduate course work in literature, journalism, and public relations.

Rob writes a popular column about 2-year college issues for *The Chronicle of Higher Education* and is also a weekly "Lifestyles" columnist for the Gwinnett Daily Post, a large suburban Atlanta newspaper. His essays and poems have appeared in a variety of other outlets, including *The Clearing House, Southern Poetry Review, The Knoxville News-Sentinel,* and the *Atlanta Journal-Constitution.*

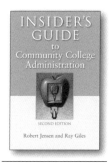